D1287913

Financial Statement Analysis Simplified

An accounting book for non-accountants

Financial Statement Analysis Simplified

Mike Morley, CPA

Nixon-Carre Ltd., Toronto, ON

Library and Archives Canada Cataloguing in Publication

Morley, Michel, 1952-
  Financial statement analysis simplified : an account-ing book for non-accountants / Michel Morley.

Includes index.
ISBN 978-0-9737470-5-8

  1. Financial statements. 2. Accounting. I. Title.
HF5681.B2M67 2009   657'.3   C2008-906352-X

Published by Nixon-Carre Ltd.
P.O. Box 92533
Carlton RPO
Toronto, Ontario, M5A 4N9
www.nixon-carre.com

Distributed by Ingram 1-800-937-8000
www.ingrambook.com

Printed and bound in the USA

Contents

Part 1 - The Basics of Accounting

v

Part 2 - The Components of Financial Statements

Part 3 - Practice Cases

Part 1

The Basics of Accounting

Why Analyze Financial Statements? 1

Financial statement analysis can really pay off

Careful analysis of Enron's financial statements, in particular the notes, led to a windfall for a hedge-fund manager named James Chanos. According to the book "Enron: The Smartest Guys in the Room" by Bethany McLean and Peter Elkind, while reading Enron's financial statement notes, Chanos spotted the fuzzy references to "related party" transactions involving Enron's senior officers, and extensive insider selling. In 2000, a full year before Enron went broke, he shorted the stock and made a tidy profit for himself and his clients.

But you don't have to be a hedge fund manager to reap the benefits of financial statement analysis. Anyone can use the same techniques to look for clues that point to possible problem areas. Business owners, managers, executives also use this analysis to see where they can reduce costs and increase profits. Financial statement analysis is a tool used to measure many different ratios such as return on investment or net income. In particular, business owners and executives should continually monitor ratios to ensure that their company is not in breach of its loan covenants. Otherwise, if certain ratios, such as the working capital (current assets to current liabilities) ratio or the debt-to-equity ratio are not maintained at the level set as a condition for the loan, then the bank or lender can choose to call the loan. This could force the company into a financial crisis or even bankruptcy.

Sarbanes-Oxley

The Sarbanes-Oxley Act of 2002, is a U.S. law that came into effect July 30, 2002, to strengthen corporate governance and restore investor confidence. It was enacted mainly as a response to the largest bankruptcy in United States history (Enron). The goal of the Act is to protect investors by improving the accuracy and reliability of corporate disclosures.

The Sarbanes-Oxley Act of 2002 is a brilliant and simple solution to the "I didn't know" defense. It makes CEO's and CFO's of U.S. publicly traded companies personally responsible not only for financial statements that accurately reflect the financial condition of the company, but also makes them personally responsible for setting up and maintaining systems that ensure that they know what they ought to know. For CEO's and CFO's, ignorance of what is going on in their company is no longer an excuse.

The Securities and Exchange Commission has decided that financial statement analysis is important enough to be included in their three-day course on ethics for corporate executives. The Commission has said that it strongly believes that even non-accounting executives such as business managers and general managers need to understand how financial statements work. It is vital that managers be able to interpret the data for themselves and spot any fraud or reporting errors.

As James Chanos' story illustrates, investors can use financial statement analysis to ensure that they know enough to ask the right questions. Although the numbers reveal part of the story, investors still need to read between the lines to uncover clues about vital negative information a company might hesitate to highlight.

More information about the Sarbanes-Oxley Act is available in my book **"Sarbanes-Oxley Simplified"** ISBN 978-0-9783939-5-3.

Evaluating risk

Lenders, creditors, and suppliers can also benefit by being able to evaluate the risks associated with a particular company. Some of these risks include the company's ability to continue as a going-concern, its capacity to meet its financial obligations as they fall due, maintaining sales levels, having up-to-date inventory, adequate research and development, and sufficient financing.

Although details about any particular supplier are rarely available, suppliers and lenders can figure out whether suppliers as a group are being paid on time. They can also get more information about how the company finances its activities in the notes to its financial statements.

Objective and verifiable information

The primary objective in financial statement analysis is to gather unbiased information that can be independently verified through reliable third parties, such as external credit rating and reporting agencies, or the outside auditor who signed the audited financial statements, and use this information to help you make informed decisions.

When I was working in the high-tech industry, a sales representative approached me about a prospect company that had just developed the latest in cell phone technology. The firm had secured venture capital funding and was poised to take over the market. It sounded great.

However, examining the financial statements revealed that financing was structured in such a way that the venture capital firm could pull out its money at any time and leave the company with virtually no cash and no net worth. Without looking closely at the financial statements, I would not have known this.

The sales person still insisted that the company would do well. Unfortunately, this was an opinion (founded perhaps on hopes of sales commissions?), but not a verifiable fact. Based on our review of the financial statements, we did not extend credit to this company. This turned out to be the right decision. Competing cell phone companies soon developed similar technology and our potential customer's competitive advantage quickly disappeared. The venture capital firm pulled their funding and the fledgling company was out of business.

A personality profile of management

Financial statements are a summary of the financial transactions that took place during the accounting period. Every financial transaction is the result of a decision by someone in management. A reflection of the company's policies, these decisions have an impact on the company's current and future financial condition. Therefore, looking at a financial statement is like looking at a personality profile of management. For example, the amount of detail that is provided in the notes to the statements is a reflection of management's willingness to be open with its investors and creditors. Are they just giving the minimum required by law, are they trying to hide something, or are they trying to provide complete information that will enable readers of the financial statements to make well informed decisions?

Another indicator of management's policies is the adequacy of cash reserves. If a company keeps adequate cash reserves on hand it usually indicates that the management is cautious. Whereas, if a company tends to overextend itself, it often indicates that management may be more reckless.

Tracking the performance of target companies

Benchmarking is the term used to describe the practice of setting up a system to track the performance of target companies. This is done by extracting the characteristics of the best performers and looking for those characteristics in other companies. Benchmarking can be particularly useful in sales prospecting, making investment decisions, and in making lending decisions. Financial statement analysis allows you to gather evidence to determine whether your assumptions about what makes a good prospect are correct.

The Emperor has no clothes

Perhaps you remember from your childhood the story of The Emperor's New Clothes written by Hans Christian Andersen. It went something like this:

Once upon a time there lived an emperor who was very vain and foolish, and he cared very much about his clothes. Two crooks came up with an idea to swindle some money from the emperor. They told him that they could make him the finest suit of clothes from the most beautiful cloth. This cloth, they said, also had the special feature that it was invisible to anyone who was either stupid or not fit for his position.

Being a bit nervous about whether he himself would be able to see the cloth, the emperor first sent two of his most trusted men to see it. Of course, neither of them would admit that they could not see the cloth and so praised it.

The emperor then allowed himself to be dressed in the clothes for a procession through town, never admitting that he was too unfit and stupid to see what he was wearing. Of course, all the townspeople wildly praised the magnificent clothes of the emperor, afraid to admit that they too could not see them, until a small child in the crowd said: "But he has nothing on!"

This was whispered from person to person until everyone in the crowd was shouting that the emperor had nothing on.

The moral of the story is: Just because everyone else says something is true, doesn't mean that it is.

This aspect of human nature is readily apparent in

investing and business decision-making. For example, credit professionals often feel the pressure of competitors having already approved credit limits for their customer. They often have to deal with sales people or management who do not understand why they hesitate when many other suppliers have already jumped in. The implication is that the credit department is missing something that everyone else sees.

Investors can fall into this trap as well. When the whole herd starts stampeding into the next big IPO it is tempting to run along. But you would be better to take the advice of Warren Buffet who says that he never invests in a business that he doesn't understand.

Financial statement analysis will help you make the right decisions. Evaluate the facts for yourself and do not be swayed by the fact that no one else is admitting that the Emperor has no clothes.

Where Do You Get the Information? 2

Getting the financial statements

Private companies tend to be reluctant to share financial information with suppliers and creditors. For the entrepreneur who started the company it is their baby. They have nurtured it and watched it grow and can be reluctant to share what they perceive to be their secrets. Their reluctance may sometimes be based on the perception that they can negotiate a better deal if the supplier is not aware of any possible weaknesses, now or in the future.

Private companies are not required by law to prepare financial statements that have been audited. This means that private companies will only audit their financial statements when there is a business need. This makes it unlikely that private companies will provide audited financial statements to investors, lenders and suppliers. The one exception may be the company's bank. They are usually in a position to insist on audited financial statements from private companies because they hold the collateral for their loans. Unfortunately, for other lenders and investors, the information contained in un-audited financial statements may be less reliable than those verified by an outside auditor.

Suppliers to private companies who are unable to get audited financial statements will still need to know how the company pays its bills. Hopefully the private company has released some of its financial data to credit reporting agencies (one of the best-known ones is Dun & Bradstreet). These reports may or may not include financial statement information but often include a confirmation of the corporate name and address, a list of its officers, a description of its business locations, and a short description of its business activities. Unfortunately some of this information may be outdated by the time the supplier receives the report.

Public companies are much easier to get information on since they are required by law to publish their financial statements in a timely manner. They must make them available to their shareholders and to the regulatory body governing the stock exchanges.

Late filing is a warning sign of problems

Nortel is one example of late filing being a sign that things are not what they seem. They filed for bankruptcy protection in January of 2009, following several years of late filings and accusations of accounting irregularities and restatement of several financial statements.

The Internet

The Internet is a great resource for finding financial information. Public companies are required to post their financial statements on their company web site. In addition, their submissions to the Securities and Exchange Commission (SEC) and Ontario Securities Commission (OSC) are available to the public on the SEC or OSC web sites. Anyone can access a public company's information on demand.

Private companies can keep their financial statements private, except for regulatory and tax purposes, but you can sometimes find clues about the state of the company on the Internet either through the company website or news items.

Be wary of chat rooms, "blogs", and message boards as sources of company information. Although they can be entertaining, and sometimes the information can be accurate because employees use this medium to anonymously reveal information that would not otherwise become public, these public discussion media have limited value as reliable sources of information because some people use them to instigate rumors in the hopes of manipulating the stock price.

Beware of rumors on the Internet

Issues raised by message boards and chat rooms can include inaccurate or misleading disclosures, selective disclosures, rumors, and market manipulation.

In May 1996, the stock price of Comparator Systems Corporation went from 6 cents a share to $1.88 a share in three days. During that time, more than 449 million shares of this tiny company changed hands before trading was halted. In the days preceding this flurry of trading activity, Internet chat rooms and user forums were filled with rumors about the stock. Investigators suspect that brokers and corporate insiders may have been the source of some of these rumors, presumably in an attempt to drive up the share price while the insiders sold their stock.

Internet hoaxes

PairGain, Inc., a California company, was the target of an Internet hoax. On April 7, 1999, someone posted a forged Web site that looked like part of the Bloomberg News site. The forged site announced that PairGain would be acquired by ECI Telecom Ltd., a competitor. Within minutes, PairGain's Yahoo message board referred to the bogus announcement and provided a link to the forged Web site.

This triggered a flurry of trading activity, causing PairGain's stock to rise 30 percent in the first few hours of trading. By the time the announcement was refuted several hours later, trading slowed down, but the stock still closed up 10 per cent for the day.

Nine days later, the FBI arrested and charged a 25-year-old computer engineer employed by PairGain with securities fraud for creating the forged Bloomberg News Web site. Why he did it isn't clear as the charges did not allege that he engaged in any profit-taking on the false information.

On the other hand, the Internet is a great place to keep an eye on the latest news, such as new products or possible mergers. Many individual company sites allow you to sign up to be notified automatically when news is released about their company.

In addition, you can sign up with www.Google.com or www.CNNMoney.com to receive free email alerts. You simply register and type in the name of the company you want to follow as your criteria for receiving emails.

For public filing information on U.S. companies go to:

www.edgar.com

EDGAR (Electronic Data Gathering, Analysis, and Retrieval system) allows you to retrieve real-time filings for a specific company and to find key company information - including the company name, address, telephone number, state of incorporation, Central Index Key (CIK) number, Standard Industrial Classification (SIC) code, and fiscal year end.

For public filing information on Canadian companies go to:

www.sedar.com

SEDAR (System for Electronic Document Analysis and Retrieval) is the official Canadian site that provides access to most public securities documents and information filed by public companies and investment funds with the Canadian Securities Administrators (CSA).

Industry information

There are many companies that gather and sell data by industry sector. The value of the information will vary depending on the source, and the timeliness and completeness of the data. Some of these industry-reporting services get their information by calling the subject companies to get verbal confirmation only. The danger is that this information may be biased or incomplete.

Credit rating agencies

There are three main credit rating agencies that provide ratings on larger North-American public companies: Moody's, Standard and Poor's, and Fitch Ratings. All three credit rating agencies measure the same thing: the ability of a company to produce cash in the future, and therefore the ability to meet its financial obligations as they fall due.

To establish the company's credit rating, the credit rating agencies review the company's financial statements, other information provided by the company's management, and do interviews with key personnel. Not only do the credit rating agencies examine the financial statements, but they are often able to obtain additional information which individuals might not have access to.

Keep in mind that although these credit reporting agencies sell their ratings services to current and potential creditors, they also earn revenue by encouraging the companies who are being rated to purchase additional consulting services such as reviewing the existing rating with a view to improving it. This potential for "buying the rating" was one of the factors examined as part of the investigation into the Enron scandal.

If a company has no rating, it may be because the company has not applied for a rating, because of a lack of sufficient information to issue a credit rating, or because it is a private company.

If one of the companies that you are following has a change in rating, either up or down, a review should be undertaken. Keep a particularly close eye on companies who are on the credit rating agencies' "watch lists." These are firms whose rating may be more volatile because new information is about to be released or has recently been released.

As well, all three credit rating agencies provide a "ratings outlook" which is an opinion about what the rating will be in the future.

The Building Blocks of Accounting 3

This chapter explains the principles that accountants follow in producing financial statements. Although useful to understand, this is not absolutely necessary to know in order to successfully analyze financial statements.

North American publicly traded companies are presently preparing their financial statements according to Generally Accepted Accounting Principles (GAAP), but this is quickly changing. Canada is moving to IFRS (International Financial Reporting Standards) based statements effective January 1, 2011, and the chairman of the SEC has announced that the U.S.A. will be switching over by 2014.

GAAP has been with us for many years and is not being abandoned. GAAP will continue to be used for some time after the official switch to IFRS.

More details about IFRS are in my book **"IFRS Simplified"** ISBN 978-0-9783939-1-5.

GAAP: The basic building blocks

GAAP means generally accepted accounting principles. The governing accounting bodies in the U.S.A., Canada, and Europe set these principles. These principles are the guidelines that must be followed in preparing financial statements. Having a standard way of preparing financial statements allows the users of statements to understand them, and to compare year-to-year statements as well as compare the statements of different companies.

U.S.A. GAAP vs. Canadian GAAP

Although U.S. and Canadian GAAP are essentially the same, there are a few differences that may or may not be significant in the financial statement that you are evaluating.

One of the largest assets on a company's balance sheet is Inventory, and one of the differences between U.S. GAAP and Canadian GAAP involves how and when to record inventory that is obsolete, and how to value the inventory on hand. In Canada when the inventory becomes obsolete it is written off. In the U.S. a company may choose to follow the same method as in Canada, or they may choose to establish a reserve for obsolete inventory.

During the "dotcom era", companies often manipulated their obsolescence reserve to smooth out "bumps" in earnings, by taking "one-time" charges.

Another primary difference is the depreciation of assets using different schedules. For example, a particular class or group of buildings in Canada may be depreciated over 20 years while the same class of buildings in the U.S. might be depreciated over 15 years, depending on the rules at the time. This will affect the depreciation expense, balance sheet, and net income figures.

Short-term investments

Under U.S. GAAP, short-term investments are recorded at their fair market value. Canadian companies record short-term investments at the lower of cost or market value. This difference could be significant to the investor who is trying to compare the investment income of a Canadian company to that of a U.S. company.

Long-term portfolio investments

U.S. companies record long-term investments at market value. Canadian companies, on the other hand, record long-term investments at their cost. How the long-term investments are recorded could have an impact on the income statement depending on whether they had increased or decreased in value.

GAAS

Accounting and auditing regulatory bodies set "Generally Accepted Auditing Standards" (GAAS) used by auditors in preparing audited financial statements. These standards outline how audits are to be performed and what procedures are to be followed when irregularities are found.

Maintaining the independence of the auditor is critical to providing reliable financial disclosures to investors, lenders, and suppliers.

GAAP vs. IFRS (Europe)

U.S. and Canadian GAAP are not the same as the International Accounting Standards used in Europe. The difference lies in the latitude given accountants and auditors in exercising their judgment on how a particular item is accounted for and presented in the financial statements.

In Europe, accountants and companies follow what used to be called "International Accounting Standards" (IAS). These standards have been renamed "International Financial Reporting Standards" (IFRS).

IFRS serve the same function as GAAP: they are guidelines for accountants and companies in preparing financial statements. Although they have the same goals, the approach is different.

Since the enactment of The Sarbanes-Oxley Act of 2002, U.S. GAAP has become much more rules based than previously, setting out very detailed and precise rules for very specific accounting problems. In contrast, IFRS are principle-based, providing more general guidelines.

Proponents of IFRS say that Sarbanes-Oxley and U.S. GAAP leave no room for common sense decisions in interpreting the rules. Defenders of U.S. GAAP counter that the interpretation of accounting principles is very subjective and makes it even easier for companies to manipulate their financial information.

As companies become more global, they seek to be traded on international stock exchanges. This has created pressure to come up with a global set of accounting principles that will help investors to compare the financial statements of multi-national companies more easily.

The emphasis of this book is cash flow

The switchover to IFRS will not change the basic methods of financial statement analysis as presented in this book. This book emphasizes analysis based on cash flow since for lenders and investors the most important piece of information they need to know is whether a company can pay its bills and stay in business.

Otherwise profitable companies can go bankrupt when they run out of cash, so for most purposes financial statement analysis should focus on the cash cycle of companies. The cash cycle is the number of days from the time the company first invests its money in inventory or in the providing of services, sells and bills the items or services (accounts receivable) to its customers, collects the money from them, and has cash available again to pay for the inventory it bought or services it paid for in the first place (accounts payable).

Not only is a company's cash cycle a valuable indicator of a company's ability to pay its obligations to lenders as they fall due, but it also measures the company's capacity to take advantage of other opportunities that may provide a greater return for its investors.

Generally Accepted Accounting Principles

Going-concern

It is understood that the company is a "going concern." In other words, it is being run to be profitable and to stay in business forever. This assumes that no decisions are being made with a view to shutting down the company.

Materiality

The materiality principle says that an exception can be made to a rule as long as the reader's ability to judge the financial statements is not impaired by the exception. For example, a $50 sale missing from a $10 billion dollar company's sales figures would not be significant in the overall scheme of things. In other words, it will not materially affect decisions based on the information contained in the financial statements.

Changes in accounting policy

Auditors look for significant changes in accounts from period to period. These changes can occur as a result of a change in the number and size of financial transactions, or as a result of a change in how things are measured, which is called a change in accounting policy. Significant changes in accounting policy must be disclosed in the notes to the financial statements. For example, it is common for a company to revise its depreciation policy because the expected useful life of assets has changed, and to disclose this significant (material) change in the notes to the financial statements.

Matching principle

The matching principle states that each expense item must be recorded in the same accounting period as the revenue it helped to earn. If this is not done, the financial statements will not report the results of operations accurately.

Conservatism

The principle of conservatism requires that accountants make evaluations and estimates, and select procedures that result in producing financial statements that neither overstate nor understate the company's financial condition.

The high tech bubble of the 1990's saw many companies taking "one-time charges" on their quarterly reports when profits were good and avoiding them when profits were down. There was a lot of pressure to "meet or beat the street" and the companies adjusted the numbers accordingly. Unwarranted manipulation produced large bonuses and stock option gains for many company executives.

Historical cost

The cost principle states that assets and liabilities must be recorded at their cost. This is the figure that appears on the source document for the transaction, such as an invoice. The value recorded for an asset is not altered if the market value of the asset changes. It would take an entirely new transaction based on new objective evidence to change the original value of an asset.

There are times when objective evidence is simply not

available. For example, if a building is inherited, the transaction is recorded at the building's fair market value, which must be verified and documented by reliable and independent means.

The business entity concept

The business entity concept provides that the accounting for a business or organization be kept separate from the personal affairs of its owners, shareholders, or from any other business or organization. The financial statements of the business must reflect the financial position of the business alone.

The objectivity principle

The objectivity principle says that financial transactions must be recorded based on objective evidence. The source document for a transaction is almost always the best objective evidence available, because it shows the amount agreed to by the buyer and the seller.

Revenue recognition

Revenue must be recorded (recognized) at the time the transaction is completed. Revenue can be taken into the accounts on a periodic basis, such as in the case of a long-lasting project like the construction of a building where payments are received over time.

However, it is very tempting to recognize revenue when it should not be because of the favorable impact it has on the share price of publicly traded companies.

In July 25, 2007, ConAgra Foods agreed to pay $45

million to settle SEC allegations that it engaged in improper and fraudulent accounting practices. The SEC accused the food company of improper and premature revenue recognition. In particular, the SEC alleged that from 2002 to 2005, ConAgra's corporate tax department made numerous tax errors, causing the company to improperly account for tax benefits and understate its income tax expense and overstate its net income. ConAgra misstated its reported income before income taxes by nearly $218.5 million, according to the SEC.

The company restated its financial statements for the years 1999 through 2005, and consented to a review by an independent consultant of its policies and procedures and financial and accounting compliance functions.

The consistency principle

The consistency principle requires that the same methods and procedures be applied in every accounting period. A change in method from one period to another must be explained clearly in the notes to the financial statements. The readers of financial statements have the right to assume that consistency has been applied if there is no statement to the contrary. The consistency principle aims at preventing companies from changing methods for the sole purpose of manipulating figures on their financial statements.

The full disclosure principle

The full disclosure principle says that any and all information that affects the full understanding of a company's financial condition must be included with the financial statements. Information about items that might not otherwise be obvious to the reader should be included in the form of accompanying notes. Examples of such items are outstanding lawsuits, tax disputes, contingent liabilities, and company takeovers.

The double-entry system

The double-entry system is the basic building block of accounting. I am explaining it here so that you understand how the financial statements are created, but you will never see the actual journal entries. The double-entry system is used to record transactions. The financial statements are a summary of the financial transactions.

It is called "double" because every financial transaction is recorded in at least two accounts. Each account is either a "debit" account or a "credit" account. Because these accounts look like a "T" in accounting course books, they often are called "T-accounts." Each has a left side (debit) and a right side (credit). They are organized into a "chart of accounts." The chart of accounts is a computerized roadmap that groups the accounts by account number so that they mirror the order in which they will appear in the financial statements.

For each financial transaction, the total of the "debits" must equal the total of the "credits". This is referred to as "balancing". In fact, the process of preparing financial statements includes the preparation of a "trial balance" to make sure all the credits and debits are equal for all the financial transactions recorded in an accounting period. This preliminary "balancing" procedure ensures that no entries or accounts have been forgotten.

In the financial statements, debit items (assets) are listed on the left side of the balance sheet and credit items (liabilities and equity) are listed on the right side of the balance sheet. The total of all the debits (assets) "balances" the total of all the credits (liabilities and equity).

Recording debits and credits in the accounts

An increase in an asset account means a debit entry or left side of the "T-account" while a decrease means a credit entry or right side of the "T-account."

An increase in liability or equity account means a credit entry and a decrease means a debit entry. Regardless of how many accounts are affected by a single financial transaction, all debits and credits should be equal for that transaction. Again, the trial balance verifies that the total of all debits equals the total of all credits for the accounting period.

Even a few cents difference can be significant. For example, the amounts may be out by $1 million dollars on the debit side, and out by $999,999.99 on the credit side. These significant differences can be masked by a net difference of only a single penny. Every discrepancy has to be carefully reviewed.

The Double-Entry System

Debit	Credit

Debits and Credits

Debit accounts

- Debit accounts are used to record the acquisition of assets, such as the purchase of a building. The transaction is recorded by entering the value of the purchased asset on the left side (debit) of the asset account, and a corresponding entry on the right side (credit) of another asset account, such as cash, or the right side (credit) of a liability account, such as a mortgage payable. All the debits and all the credits for each transaction must balance.

For example, the purchase of a building for cash means a credit to the cash account (reduction of cash) and a debit to the buildings account (increase in buildings). The purchase of the same building by putting a down payment in cash and getting a mortgage means a debit to the buildings account (increase in buildings), a credit to the cash account and a credit to the mortgages payable account (increase in mortgages payable).

Purchase of a building for cash:

Building		Cash	
100,000			100,000

Purchase of a building by getting a mortgage:

Building		Cash		Mortgage	
100,000			20,000		80,000

Credit accounts

Credit accounts are used to record the incurring of liabilities, such as the purchase of inventory on credit. The transaction is recorded by entering the value of the purchased inventory on the left side (debit) of the asset account (inventory), and a corresponding entry on the right side (credit) of a liability account, usually accounts payable.

Credit accounts are also used to record the investments by shareholders (equity), and profits that are not distributed as dividends (retained earnings). Credit accounts are found on the right side of the balance sheet. All the debits and all the credits for each transaction must balance.

Accrual vs. cash basis

Recording transactions on a "cash basis" means that transactions are recorded only when cash is received and when cash is paid out.

Recording transactions on an "accrual basis" means that the benefits received from financial transactions are recorded in the accounting period in which those benefits are received, regardless of when the cash payment for those benefits was made, and costs are recorded when the liability is incurred, regardless of when the bill is actually paid. For example, insurance premiums may be paid once a year, but the benefits accrue all year, and the cost of insurance is recorded evenly throughout the year, usually on a monthly basis.

Another example of the accrual basis of accounting is including credit sales in the month the sale was made, not when the cash is collected.

Although sole proprietors may have the option to use either the cash or accrual basis of accounting, other forms of business organization do not have that option. They are obligated to use the accrual basis of accounting.

Different Types of Financial Statements

4

There are several types of financial statements, depending on the purpose for which they were prepared. These include statements prepared for tax filings, for managing a company, for internal and external reports, and for evaluating possible future circumstances (what-if scenarios).

Financial statements prepared for tax filing purposes

Businesses are required to include a financial statement when they complete their annual tax return. Financial statements prepared for tax return purposes often differ from other types of financial statements. Tax laws stipulate how particular transactions must be reported. For example, tax laws dictate in which period certain revenues and expenses are reported, and how depreciation expense and deferring of revenue must be reported. These differences are called "timing differences."

Preparing different financial statements for tax purposes is not fraudulent. These are only timing differences. Companies are not only entitled to take advantage of favorable tax laws, they have an obligation to reduce taxes and increase profits for their shareholders.

Corporations can use losses in previous years to reduce the tax on future profits and those of the current year. In addition, some jurisdictions allow companies to go back and claim back taxes paid in prior periods. In some cases, the tax laws may even allow small business owners to report significantly less income for tax purposes than they actually take in.

A potential investor in a private company should ask to see the financial statements prepared for tax purposes. Tax liabilities or tax credits on the statements could make companies valuable. Companies with substantial unused deferred tax credits can become takeover targets for companies looking to reduce the amount of corporate tax they pay and improve their cash flow.

Financial statements prepared for management

Financial statements that are put together to help management run the company tend to focus on profitability, costs, and the overall return on investment for shareholders. These kinds of financial statements can be used to compare actual results against the budget that was prepared at the beginning of the year.

Company management relies heavily on ongoing internal financial reports and statements to keep an eye on the company's performance. These internal reports can point out areas that are not keeping up to expectations. With constant, up-to-the-minute feedback, managers can make adjustments quickly. This makes better use of assets and increases the return on invested capital.

Internal reporting

Internal financial reports are prepared for the exclusive use of the company and its employees. Because they are not released to the public and therefore do not have to be based on generally accepted accounting principles or any other rules imposed by regulators, these internal reports provide only limited value to outsiders.

External reporting

Financial statements prepared for external reporting purposes must follow generally accepted accounting principles and other strict rules imposed by regulatory bodies, such as the Securities and Exchange Commission. One of these GAAP principles, the "historical cost" principle, says that "historical" numbers must be used. In other words, these financial statements are always looking at events in the past. Because these "historical" amounts must have supporting documents, such as original invoices, uncertainty about the historical costs being reported in the financial statements is reduced.

Pro-forma financial statements

Pro-forma financial statements are "forward-looking". Unlike "historical" statements which show what happened in the past, pro-forma statements show what the company predicts will happen in the future. While still required to use GAAP, many companies prepare pro-forma financial statements to see what the results would be if certain assumptions are made. These assumptions could include an increase in revenue, the introduction of a new product or service, the acquisition of another firm, etc. These assumptions, as required by the

Sarbanes-Oxley Act of 2002 in the United States, must be spelled out in easy-to-understand language so that the readers of the financial statements have no doubt that they are looking at "forward-looking" pro-forma financial statements, not historical "past-looking" financial statements and what underlying assumptions are being used.

In the high-tech bubble of the nineties, pro-forma statements were used to entice investors. By assuming that projected increases in revenue would continue exponentially as they had in the recent couple of years, companies would forecast this unrealistic growth many years ahead in their pro-forma financial statements. In the feeding frenzy of the high-tech stock market, many investors did not take the time to understand that the pro-forma financial statements relied on unrealistic assumptions. They lost their money when the stock price increases could not be sustained.

Even back in 2001, the SEC was clear that it would crack down on misleading information in pro-forma financial statements when it issued "cautionary advice" that companies and their advisors should consider when releasing pro forma financial information. The SEC reminded investors that pro-forma financial statements should be viewed with "appropriate and healthy skepticism."

The entrepreneurial mindset

Entrepreneurs tend to be optimistic and self-confident business people. They see the "big picture" and are often not as concerned with the details. Of course this is a generalization, but understanding the personality of an entrepreneur helps you to have a better perspective particularly where future projections are concerned.

Consolidated statements

Consolidated financial statements include all the financial information related to all the subsidiaries and divisions of the company. For example, if a company has many diversified subsidiary companies even in unrelated business sectors, the consolidated statements of the "mother" company contain all of the financial information of all these businesses combined. Even though you are looking at a particular division or subsidiary, the consolidated company will be influencing the financial decisions by setting overall financial policy. So it is important that you get the company's consolidated financial statements.

Public companies must file their consolidated financial statements. Profits can be transferred via inter-company transactions, but must be netted out in the consolidated financial statements.

Other reports

Accountants prepare other reports in addition to preparing financial statements:

Compilations

Compilations are simply the calculation and tidying up of accounts and numbers into an organized list. Except for the numerical accuracy of the report, the accountant preparing the compilation does not make any judgment about the validity of the report.

Reviews

In this kind of report, the accountant looks at the numbers and presents a limited opinion about their validity. In other words, it is a "sanity check" to make sure nothing seems out of kilter. The accountant does not verify any supporting documentation to determine if the numbers reflect the reality of the financial transactions. A review assumes that the numbers that were recorded were correct in the first place.

Audits

Audits require that the auditor not only review the numbers, but that tests are performed to make sure those transactions are recorded correctly and follow generally accepted accounting principles. Audits are mandatory for publicly traded companies. In the U.S. Certified Public Accountants (CPA's) perform audits; in Canada, at the present time, although there are three regulating bodies for accountants, Chartered Accountants perform the majority of audits.

Re-evaluating Financial Statements

5

Policy

Any investor or creditor should have a policy in place that clearly states what criteria would trigger a financial statement review. Criteria you can use include late payment, rumors, mergers and acquisitions, market conditions, changes in patterns, and time.

Your policy for these triggers and the timing of these reviews would depend on what use you are making of the information. For example, if you are a creditor, you want to know if there is a reduction in cash flow which might mean you may not receive your money in full or on time. On the other hand, if you are an investor, the selling of shares by executives is a sign that should cause you to find out what is prompting them to sell. Perhaps you should do the same.

Late payment

If the customer starts paying late, something has changed, and the previous assessment may no longer be valid. For example, if sales are slowing down because of material shortages, then the company will not have the revenue they were counting on to pay their bills. You need to ascertain if this is only a temporary situation, or a longer term issue. You need to find out if the company has plans to deal with this potential financial crisis. Another example might be that the company is deliberately slowing down payments to bolster working capital for its quarter-end. They might be concerned about meeting their bank loan covenants and having the bank call in their loan (demand immediate full payment).

Some companies deliberately stop paying their bills about two weeks before quarter end, while at the same time pushing hard to collect as much of their accounts receivable as they possibly can. This combination allows them to build up cash for their quarter end. The reason they do this is to ensure that they can meet bank covenants.

Bank covenants are conditions imposed by a financial institution when extending credit to a company. Often one of these covenants requires a minimum amount of cash on hand at all times. If the bank does not see the minimum amount of cash on hand at the end of the quarter it can call the company's loan, requiring immediate full payment.

Unfortunately, this form of cash management relies on the goodwill of the suppliers and their willingness to continue shipping product or providing services even when their account is late. The company is risking that the supplier will not wait for their payment and shipments may be halted until the account is brought up to date.

So some companies with strong cash balances do not necessarily have their accounts paid up to date. The financial statements should be closely examined to see if the accounts payable are being paid on a regular basis. It could be that the cash on hand will disappear quickly after the end of the quarter when accounts payable payments are caught up.

Increase in deductions

Another sign of trouble is an increase in deductions, disputes, and legal actions. Disputes are a common delaying tactic for hiding cash flow problems. Disputes are public knowledge if they are being fought out in court. On the other hand, it is more difficult to ascertain how many creditors are receiving deductions, since each creditor is only aware of the extent of their own deductions.

If creditors share their credit experience, especially in a particular industry, then they may suspect something is going on, but probably can only guess at exactly how big the problem really is. Companies do have legitimate disputes with suppliers from time to time. However, it is hard to believe that they would have problems with all their suppliers at the same time. If many of the creditors are noticing an increase in deductions something is wrong.

I remember one company making regular deductions from accounts payable in order to conserve cash. I recall visiting the comptroller's office and noticing a large number of checks on his credenza behind his desk. When I asked him why he had such a large number of unsigned checks behind him, he replied that he would pay the bills for those suppliers after they called him back saying that his request for a credit note was denied. In other words he anticipated the refusal but in the meantime was able to hang on to his cash.

Rumors

If you hear rumors, investigate them immediately to make sure that you are not missing an early warning. Remember the old expression "Where there's smoke, there's fire." Rumors usually start for a reason.

Persistent rumors should always be investigated to determine their validity and potential effect. It could be a signal to buy or to sell. For example, rumors about Nortel's imminent demise have been around for years. The company finally sought bankruptcy protection in early 2009.

Market conditions

When market conditions change, the company's sales may be affected. If sales go down, future cash flow may be reduced. If sales increase substantially, the expansion may strain the company's working capital, especially cash. This may mean a slow down in payments. You need to evaluate the potential effects of the change in market conditions on the company's ability to pay bills on time.

Changes in pattern

Any change in the pattern of how the company does business should alert you to something going on. For example, if the company has increased its purchases from one supplier, it could be that those sales people are doing a great job, or it could also be that another supplier has cut them off. Confirm the real reason for the change.

Time

Regular reviews need to be done simply because time has gone by. The situation may have changed and you need to ascertain if the company still meets your criteria. A change in financial condition may expose opportunities or risks.

The hidden risks of mergers and acquisitions

If the company is looking to acquire or merge with another company, the financial landscape may change drastically, and it can literally happen overnight. The company's management may no longer be in control, and the new management's financial policy may no longer meet your criteria.

What is the company really buying?

Merger and acquisition talks are usually held in secret. The acquiring company tries to get as much information as possible about a company it wants to take over. However, there may be legal restrictions on the amount information that can be shared, especially if the two companies are in the same industry. So the buyer never fully knows what they are getting until the sale is final and they have access to all the purchased company's information and files.

For example, Maytag was acquired by Whirlpool in March of 2006. Because both companies were in the appliance industry, the Securities and Exchange Commission allowed only limited access by Whirlpool to Maytag's books and other information, to protect Maytag in the event that the sale did not go through. Only after the sale went through on March 31, 2006, did Whirlpool really find out what it had purchased.

Some acquired companies may have hidden cash flow problems that end up being inherited by the purchasing company. A previously good-paying, low-risk customer, may temporarily at least, not be able to meet financial commitments.

Process and systems incompatibility

In a merger, one primary issue is the incompatibility of systems and processes. Management has three choices: 1) to change the acquired company's system to its own, 2) to adopt the acquired company's system, or 3) to design a new one.

Sarbanes-Oxley/Bill 198

Sarbanes-Oxley (and Bill 198 in Canada) has changed the landscape of mergers and acquisitions involving public companies. Target companies must become Sarbanes-Oxley/Bill 198 compliant as their financial disclosures become part of the purchasing company's consolidated financial statements. Many companies claim to be compliant but on closer scrutiny they are not. Unfortunately, company outsiders can not verify this by looking at the financial statements

The importance of a consistent methodology

Developing a consistent methodology for financial statement analysis means that you do it the same way every time with every company. This makes it unlikely that you will forget any steps.

It also enables you to compare one company to another in an industry group. Such comparisons can be used to set benchmarks for predicting probable performance and future risk. These comparisons can be used to establish a scoring system to facilitate and speed up your decision making process.

Other items to watch for

Some of the specific issues that you need to watch for include: one-time charges, investment gains, revenue recognition, timing issues, stock options and EBITDA.

One-time charges

One-time charges are expenses that a company recognizes, usually when profits are higher, that are not expected to recur. These can include merger and acquisition expenses, write-downs of obsolete inventory, and reorganization costs. One-time charges need to be closely examined for their effect on cash flow.

Companies are often tempted to manipulate the timing of one-time charges to influence the stock price. For example, in a down quarter companies might delay writing down obsolete inventory and recording the resulting loss in the hope that the next quarter will be a better time to do it. Other times, when there is a lot of bad news, the company might decide to throw in everything that could possibly look bad hoping to make the next quarter look like it has improved substantially.

Investment gains

Investment gains are accounting entries that reflect the increase in market value of the company's investments, such as stocks, bonds, and other companies. However, these accounting entries do not produce cash, and will be reversed if the market value subsequently diminishes.

Revenue recognition

When and how much revenue is recorded (recognized) is a major concern. For example, if a customer agrees to being billed for product that will be delivered only the following quarter, then a sale has not really occurred. The sales figure is inflated, along with net income and accounts receivable. However, because this future sale will not produce cash for several months, the company may not have the funds available to meet its obligations on time.

Timing issues

The timing of revenue and expense recognition is critical because it affects both net income and the balance sheet. Overhead expenses such as insurance, rent, and depreciation need to follow the matching principle to prevent overstating or understating net income and the balance sheet.

Stock options

Accounting for stock options used as executive performance incentives has become a big issue for companies that grant them. Stock options should be recorded on the financial statements as an expense if they are granted at a price lower than market price. The difference between the current market price and the stock option price is a direct benefit to employees. This difference should be treated as compensation, and the expense, along with the cost of any related benefits, should be recorded on the financial statements. In addition, there should be a detailed disclosure in the notes to the financial statements.

Both the SEC and the OSC (Ontario Stock Exchange) have recently fined and settled with executives of RIM (famous for its Blackberry) for falsely back dating stock options so that the executives received "in-the-money" options. The Commissions said the executives knew they were not supposed to do it, did it anyway, and tried to hide it from regulators and investigators. The amounts of the fines and the terms of the settlement were not disclosed.

Securities and Exchange Commission chairman Christopher Cox said in February 2007 that the Commission was investigating over 100 companies for backdating stock options.

Pension plan liability

In the past few years pension plan liability has become an important item to watch for because many large companies that have been in business for years have very large shortfalls in the amount set aside for pension plans. In the past, most pension plans were "defined benefit" plans which spelled out how much pension an employee would receive after retiring. Some companies played around with the pension fund money, using it to pay operating expenses and did not have enough money set aside to pay retirees.

If there is a shortfall between the pension plan's estimated required future payments and the amount that the actuaries calculate will be available in the plan, the company is liable for topping up the fund, and this liability must be

47

reported on the balance sheet. In the past, companies did not have to disclose this liability on the balance sheet, they were only required to put a note in their financial statements.

Even for companies that set the money aside, stock market declines of the past few years have resulted in less money in the pension fund.

This is a sleeping giant. The problem is so huge that it threatens to undermine the stability of the financial markets now and into the future. Merrill Lynch and Bloomberg estimate that the top 40 companies have defined pension liabilities of over $100 billion.

The SEC and other regulatory bodies are keeping a close eye on the pension plan liability that companies report on their financial statements. Several major companies such as Dell, AON, and GM have been forced to restate their financial statements due to these pension plan liabilities.

EBITDA

EBITDA stands for earnings before interest, taxes, depreciation, and amortization. It is a common benchmark used to compare operating performance among companies in a given sector. However, keep in mind that this is only an accounting measurement, not a measurement of cash flow, which is a better indicator of a company's ability to meet its financial commitments as they fall due.

Part 2

The Components of Financial Statements

Financial Statements are made up of the following components:

The Company Page

Management Discussion and Analysis

Audit Report

Balance Sheet

Income Statement

Statement of Changes in Financial Position
or Cash Flow Statement

Statement of Retained Earnings

Notes to the Financial Statements

The Company Page

6

On the front page you will find the name of the company, the name of the report, and the time period covered by the financial report.

The name of the company

The name of the company on the front page of the financial statements should be exactly the same as the name of the company whose report you want to examine. Even a slight difference in name can mean that you are looking at information that belongs to a completely different company.

The difference can be as small as "Company X Inc." vs. "Company X Corp." In my experience in looking at thousands of financial statements, I can tell you that I quickly learned to double-check the name. It can be an expensive lesson to learn.

I remember early in my career spending three long days gathering and analyzing information about a company. Eventually I noticed that the name on the reports were slightly different. After wasting my time (and my employer's money) I discovered that the company I should have been analyzing was a subsidiary with no assets to its name.

If the name is close, you should ask yourself "What is the relationship between the company I want to find out more about, and the company whose financial statements I have been offered? The different name is key because the value of the assets may be very different and may influence your decision, to invest in, lend to, or buy the company.

For example, when giving credit to a subsidiary, a lender, unless they have a specific guarantee from the parent company, does not have recourse to the assets of the parent company. Although the names may be close, the pool of assets available to satisfy debts can be very different.

For example, Walt Disney Pictures is a subsidiary of the Walt Disney Studio Entertainment. This means that unless Walt Disney Studio Entertainment guarantees payment of the debts of Walt Disney Pictures, then creditors of Walt Disney Pictures cannot touch the assets of Walt Disney Studio Entertainment.

It is an all too common ploy for con artists to give their company a name that is close to that of another successful company with the intention of fraudulently running up bills based on the legitimate company's financial statements. They will get goods from companies by posing as well known companies, but have the products shipped elsewhere. The products are sold for cash and the supplier never gets paid. Due diligence is the only defense against such a scheme. Verifying and documenting thoroughly will eliminate the embarrassment and cost of falling prey to these smooth operators.

Corporate identity theft is much more prevalent than

most people realize. Companies are reluctant to reveal that they are victims, and wish to protect their reputation with suppliers and customers.

The name of the report

Make sure that you have the type of report that you are looking for. For example, if you want a full year's set of financial statements, make sure that this is what you have got. The front page should say "Annual Report." Any other name on the report should alert you that you might not have received what you thought you were getting.

The time period of the report should cover the period you are interested in. If it says "Annual Report 2006," it will cover the year ending some time in 2006. If it says "Quarterly Report March 2006" it will cover the three months from January 2006 to March 31, 2006.

Reports should be produced in a reasonable time after the end of the accounting period. Year-end statements should be ready about 2 to 3 months after the books are closed. Any greater delay might be a sign of a bigger problem. If investors and lenders are offered older financial statements because the current ones are taking too long, they should be wary and ask questions. The excuse that the accountant is taking a long time is not acceptable.

What about partial financial statements?

Make sure that you receive a complete set of financial statements. If the reader of the financial statements has not received the full documentation associated with the financial statements, such as some of the "Notes to the Financial Statements", there may be limited value in reading the statements. It is like reading a book that is missing some of its pages, or trying to piece together a jigsaw puzzle that is missing pieces. You just don't know what you are missing.

Here is a simple example of a company page for an annual report:

Company XYZ

Annual Report

December 31, 2008

Management Discussion & Analysis 7

Many audited statements contain a report called "Management Discussion and Analysis." Although common practice is to include it as part of the annual report, it can be presented as a separate item. A management discussion and analysis (MD&A) report is required by all public companies in the United States and Canada.

Although management provides the management discussion and analysis, the auditor does not audit the information included in the management discussion and analysis report. Only management is accountable for this particular report, not the auditor.

The management discussion and analysis report gives management's analysis of the results of the current financial statements. The report is an opportunity for management to provide insight into its intentions, using both quantitative and qualitative methods. Quantitative methods involve numbers, such as talking about new and prospective financing. Qualitative methods include management's subjective opinion about the prospects for the company's new product being introduced in the coming year and its expected impact on sales.

Management's credibility

Readers of the management discussion and analysis report should evaluate the candor and accuracy of management's comments in the report. It is a matter of credibility. Management is trying to establish trust in order to get lenders and investors to provide funds to the company. If management is honest and does not downplay the dangers nor overstate the prospects, and can support its position using facts and solid reasoning, then it is easier for investors to trust that management will run the company in the same straightforward manner and keep the investors' best interests at heart.

Trends

Management should talk about the trends over the last couple of years and whether they are expected to continue. They should provide supporting evidence for their claims. Readers of the financial statements should be cautious about unsubstantiated claims. They are usually a result of poor research or a sign of uncertainty. For example, if management is saying that their new product will steal market share from their competitor and double sales, is there evidence being presented, perhaps in the form of one or more strong, independent, easy-to-understand market surveys, to support what management is predicting? Or are they hoping to dazzle investors with a flashy report?

The first sign that things are not what they seem is that the management discussion and analysis report is not an easy read.

Clarity

The management discussion and analysis report should be clear and easy to understand. The use of jargon should alert lenders and investors that the company may have something to hide and is attempting to confuse readers with big words.

Potential risks

Management should also disclose potential risks in the coming year or beyond. These risks, for example, might include uncertainties about markets or the supply of raw materials. Management should draw on experience, expert advice, and as much real data, as possible. The more forthcoming management is in this area, the more trust they will earn from lenders and investors.

Sarbanes-Oxley

The Sarbanes-Oxley act of 2002 requires not only that the management discussion and analysis report not be misleading, but also that management cannot omit any significant item that would have an impact on an investor's or lender's decision.

The Audit Report

8

An analyst who was working for me asked me to review his analysis of the financial statements of a prospective client company. He had just spent two full days reviewing the numbers, but still felt that something was wrong but he just could not put his finger on what it was. It turned out that he had not noticed that the audit report that accompanied the financial statements referred to a sister company with a slightly different name. I asked him to call the auditor and he found out that the auditor refused to continue the auditing engagement because of a lack of cooperation from management. The company had switched the audit report to make it look like nothing was wrong.

I still don't know exactly what they were trying to hide. In my opinion this was a clear case of fraud and we refused to do business with the company.

The important lesson here is:

Always start by looking at all the parts of the financial statements to make sure that they all refer to the company you are reviewing.

If the audit statement does not follow the usual format, or if there are any questions concerning the auditor's opinion, users of the financial statements could ask for the company's permission to discuss their concerns with the auditor. Any reluctance to have anyone talk to the auditor could be a sign that the company has something to hide.

If the contact information is not on the audit report, it can be obtained from American Institute of Certified Public Accountants or the State CPA Society, or the Canadian Institute of Chartered Accountants.

As the representative of various large companies I have seldom had any difficulty speaking to a company's auditors, but for most investors or smaller creditors the reality is that you are unlikely to have much success getting answers this way.

On one occasion when I called the State CPA Society looking for contact information you can imagine my surprise to discover that the auditor had been suspended because of improprieties. The auditor was under investigation! Needless to say, this cast doubts on the validity of the auditor's opinion and the entire financial statements.

You can speak to the company's investor relations department if you have questions about the financial statements. They will either be able to answer your questions or direct you to the person who can. It is surprisingly easy to get access to even the company CEO if the request comes through investor relations.

The auditor's opinion

It is the auditor's opinion that establishes the credibility of the company's financial statements. However, the audit report provides an opinion, not a guarantee. The auditor does not promise that the financial statements are true in every respect. The auditor reviews the financial statements submitted by management, but management is responsible for the information presented in those financial statements and management must sign the financial statements. The auditor signs the opinion.

An auditor issues an unqualified opinion when there are no apparent problems with the financial statements.

A qualified opinion is issued when the auditor feels that there is a problem with the financial statements that prevents them from issuing an unqualified opinion. In this case, the auditor will add an explanation of the issue.

Auditor's expertise

Many industries have unique accounting requirements that the auditor must understand in order to evaluate whether the company's financial statements are in accordance with generally accepted accounting principles. For example, if an auditor is doing an audit of a city's financial statements, the auditor must be familiar with governmental accounting requirements.

Some industries are more risky than others, for example oil or mining companies. They can win big, but they can also lose big if their prospecting does not find rich deposits, or if mineral or oil fields start drying up. The danger here lies in the boom or bust cycle of these companies. If you happen to be looking at financial statements in the boom cycle, the analysis must take into account how well the company can make it through bad times.

In some industries, there are some common inherent risks. Examples include potential inventory obsolescence risk, such as in the electronics industry, or in the fashion industry. Another example is the inherent accounts receivable risk in the consumer loan industry. Yet another is the casualty insurance industry where natural disasters can prove ruinous not only for the unfortunate victims, but also for the insurance companies who cannot meet the sudden need for cash payouts.

Materiality

A good way of looking at materiality is to say that something is material if it can potentially influence the investor.

Materiality is important in determining the type of opinion report that is appropriate for the current circumstances. If a misstatement is not expected to have a material effect in future periods, it is ignored. An example would be the cost of used photocopy equipment ($100) expensed in full immediately rather than carrying the unused portion on the balance sheet as capital equipment.

However, when the amounts are large enough to materially affect the financial statements, such as inventory which cannot be verified as to its quantity and value because the auditor did not supervise the physical inventory count, it should not be ignored.

Rarely is an adverse opinion issued. When the auditor warns the company's management that they are withholding information or preventing the auditor from verifying the facts as presented by management, management usually provides the auditor with what they need.

The auditor's report includes:

- Report title
- Audit report address
- Introductory paragraph
- Scope paragraph
- Opinion paragraph
- Explanatory paragraph
- Name of audit firm
- Audit report date

Report title

Generally accepted auditing standards require that the report include the word "independent." The word "independent" is intended to tell readers that the audit report was impartial. This is an important point. If the auditor is not independent, they must not accept the engagement.

Audit report address

The report is addressed to the company, its stockholders, or the board of directors. Most audit reports are addressed to stockholders. This calls attention to the fact that the auditor is independent of the company and the board of directors.

The introductory paragraph

The introductory paragraph starts by making the simple statement that the audit firm has completed an audit of the company's records. This sets the audit report apart from a compilation (putting the numbers together) or review report (an examination of the financial statements without performing a full audit). The auditor's "scope" paragraph will clarify what was done during the audit. Read this paragraph carefully to avoid mistaking a compilation or a review for an audit.

The introductory paragraph lists the types of financial statements being presented, including the balance sheet dates and the accounting periods for the income statement and statement of cash flows.

To clarify the respective roles of management and the auditor, the introductory paragraph states that management is responsible for the information being presented in the financial statements while it is the auditor's responsibility to express an opinion on the statements based on the audit.

In addition, this paragraph reminds the reader that management is responsible for selecting and applying the appropriate generally accepted accounting principles, and making all the proper disclosures. There is a danger here. The auditor relies on management to disclose all material information. Sometimes, management may want to disclose only what they absolutely have to. Fortunately, with experience, many auditors have almost a sixth sense regarding things that management is trying to cover up.

The scope paragraph

The scope paragraph says that the auditor followed generally accepted auditing standards. It outlines the auditing techniques used in the performance of the audit. The audit is designed to obtain "reasonable assurance" about whether the statements are free of "material misstatement." The word "material" underlines the fact that the auditor is responsible only to search for significant misstatements, not minor misstatements that do not affect decisions by lenders, investors, and prospective buyers. For example, a discrepancy in inventory of $3,000 will not be material to a company with sales of $500 million. However, it will be material to a company with sales of $50,000. What is material to one company may not be material to another.

The auditor uses the term "reasonable assurance" to show that an audit cannot be expected to completely remove the possibility that a material misstatement will be in the financial statements. In other words, an audit is intended to deliver a high level of assurance, but it is not a guarantee.

I recall one company CEO who tried to assure me that the auditors had "made sure" that his company was free of all fraud. I tried to explain to him that the auditors only provide reasonable assurance. Unfortunately, later that year, he found out that one of his executives had embezzled close to $150,000.

The scope paragraph will also say something about the audit evidence accumulated. It will also say that the auditor believes that the audit process provided a reasonable basis for the opinion.

When the words "test basis" are used, it means that sampling was used rather than an audit of every transaction and amount on the financial statements. Auditors do not audit every transaction. They use sampling to satisfy themselves that if things went well in the sample, chances are pretty good that things went well in most of the transactions. Otherwise, the cost of auditing would be prohibitive and would take too long.

I am continually being asked if an audit means that all the accounts have been verified. I have to reply that it does so only to the extent that the auditor is satisfied that the tests performed provide reasonable assurance that there are no material misstatements.

Opinion paragraph

The opinion paragraph presents the auditor's conclusions on the degree to which the financial statements fairly represent the company's financial position. The entire audit report is often referred to as the auditor's opinion.

As mentioned earlier, the opinion paragraph is stated as an opinion rather than as a statement of unquestionable fact. This signals to the reader that the auditor is using professional judgment. The words "in our opinion" point out that there still is some risk associated with the financial statements even though the statements have been audited.

The auditor is required to present an opinion about the financial statements taken as a whole, including a conclusion about whether generally accepted accounting principles were followed.

One of the contentious parts of the auditor's report

is the meaning of "present fairly." Sarbanes-Oxley has made auditors responsible for looking beyond generally accepted accounting principles to determine whether users might be misled, even if those principles are followed. Although most auditors believe the financial statements are presented fairly when the statements are in accordance with generally accepted accounting principles, Sarbanes-Oxley has made it also necessary for them to also look at the nature of the transaction as well as the balance when looking for possible misinformation and fraud. For example, an expense item that seems unusual, such as a payment for repairing a residential garage when the company does not own one, should be questioned. Did the principal of the company divert company funds to have his home garage fixed? The nature of the item should be examined when confirming balances for audit purposes.

An auditor once told me that a company executive was surprised that the expenditure to landscape the grounds around the corporate headquarters was questioned. The auditor had noticed the poorly maintained grounds and questioned why relatively large amounts spent on landscaping did not produce better results. The auditor followed the money trail and found out that the company executive's home was beautifully landscaped at the company's expense.

Name of the auditing firm

The name identifies the auditing firm (or individual auditor) that performed the audit. Usually, the firm's name is used, since the entire firm as well as the individual auditor has the legal and professional responsibility to make certain that the quality of the audit meets professional standards, including those imposed by Sarbanes-Oxley. Only registered

CPA (Certified Public Accountants) audit firms can perform audits in the U.S. In Canada, CA (Charted Accountants) audit firms perform audits, although some Canadian provinces, such as Quebec, allow CGA's (Certified General Accountants) to sign audits subject to provincial regulations.

Audit report date

The proper date for the report is the one on which the auditor has concluded the most important auditing procedures. The date is important to readers of the financial statements because it is the last day of the auditor's responsibility for the review of significant events that occurred after the date of the financial statements. For example, if the balance sheet is dated December 31, 2005, and the audit report is dated March 6, 2006, this means that the auditor has looked for material unrecorded transactions and events that occurred up to March 6, 2006. If a significant customer declares bankruptcy after December 31, but before March 6, the auditor has an obligation to make readers of the financial statements aware of this significant event.

Number of paragraphs

Many readers believe that the number of paragraphs in the auditor's report is an important flag as to whether the financial statements are accurate, or whether there is some exception that requires their attention. This is because the three-paragraph report usually means that there are no exceptions in the audit. The inclusion of more than three paragraphs indicates some type of explanation.

Using a second auditing firm

When the auditor uses a different auditing firm to perform part of the audit, (which is common when the client has several branches or divisions), the principal auditing firm has three alternatives:

1) No mention of the second auditing firm

This method is usually followed when the other auditor audited an immaterial portion of the statements, when the other auditor is well known or closely supervised by the principal auditor, or when the principal auditor has thoroughly reviewed the other auditor's work. The other auditor is still responsible for his or her own report and work in the event of a lawsuit or SEC action.

2) Make reference to the report (with explanatory paragraph)

This kind of report is referred to as a shared opinion and is issued when the principal auditor has not reviewed the other auditor's work that covers a material portion of the financial statements.

3) Qualify the opinion

The principal auditor may decide that a qualified opinion is needed. A qualified opinion or disclaimer, depending on materiality, is required if the principal auditor is not willing to assume any responsibility for the work of the other auditor.

Situations that prevent an unqualified (clean) audit report

There are three situations, when an unqualified audit report is not appropriate:

1) When the work of the auditor has been restricted.
2) When the financial statements have not been prepared in accordance with generally accepted accounting principles.
3) When the auditor is not independent.

Restriction of the audit

When the auditor has not gathered sufficient evidence to decide whether financial statements are prepared in accordance with GAAP, the audit is restricted. These restrictions are caused either by the client or by circumstances beyond either party's control. For example, management might refuse to allow the auditor to confirm receivables or physically count inventory.

Statements that do not follow GAAP

For example, if management insists on using market prices instead of historical cost, then generally accepted accounting principles are not followed, and the auditor should disclose this situation.

The auditor is not independent

If the auditor is not independent, the audit report cannot be issued. For example, the auditor is not independent if they are receiving other revenue from the client, such as consulting revenue.

Whenever an auditor issues a qualified report, they must use the expression "except for" in the opinion paragraph. This says that the auditor is convinced that the overall financial statements are correctly stated except for a specific aspect of them.

This would be used, for example, when a large account balance due from a customer could not be confirmed prior to the audit firm issuing its report because the customer is away on an extended business trip. Although the balance cannot be confirmed, it does not overshadow the financial statements as a whole.

Audited vs. unaudited

Financial statements that are not audited include reviews, compilations, and internal financial statements.

Reviews, which are usually prepared by an external public accountant, do not contain an audit opinion. External accountants also prepare compilations. Their job is to add up the numbers (compile). On the other hand, internal financial statements are prepared by the company's own staff. In all three cases, creditors, lenders, investors, and other readers of the financial statements, cannot rely on unaudited financial statements to the same extent as audited financial statements.

Often, these unaudited statements will contain a notice to reader. An example of this type of notice is:

We have compiled the balance sheet of "x" company as of December 31, 2008 and the statements of income, retained earnings, and changes in financial position for the year then ended from information provided by management. We have not audited, reviewed or otherwise attempted to verify the accuracy or completeness of such information. Readers are cautioned that these statements may not be appropriate for their purposes.

Audited financial statements are preferred. Ideally, you should have them going back three years. Public companies are required to publish comparative financial statements that span at least two years.

Private companies are generally not required to have their financial statements audited, however many choose to do so in order to meet banking and creditor requirements.

Example of un-qualified opinion:

To the shareholders of "x" company

We have audited the balance sheet of "x" company as at December 31, 2008 and the statements of income, retained earnings, and changes in financial position for the year then ended. These financial statements are the responsibility of the company's management. Our responsibility is to express an opinion on these financial statements based on our audit.

We conducted our audit in accordance with generally accepted auditing standards. These standards require that we plan and perform an audit to obtain reasonable assurance whether the financial statements are free of material misstatement. An audit includes examining, on a test basis, evidence supporting the amounts and disclosures in the financial statements. An audit also includes assessing the accounting principles used in significant estimates made by management, as well as evaluating the overall financial statement presentation.

In our opinion, these financial statements present fairly, in all material respects, the financial position of the company as at December 31, 2008 and the results of its operations and the changes in its financial position for the year then ended in accordance with generally accepted accounting principles.

ABC Chartered Accountants

Toronto, Ontario
March 15, 2009

Example of a qualified opinion paragraph

In our opinion, except for the effects of a failure to record depreciation as described in the preceding paragraph, these financial statements present fairly, in all material respects, the financial position of the company as at December 31, 2008 and the results of its operations and changes in its financial position for the year then ended in accordance with generally accepted accounting principles.

Example of a denial opinion paragraph

In view of the possible material effects on the financial statements of the matters described in the preceding paragraph, we are unable to express an opinion whether these financial statements are presented in accordance with generally accepted accounting principles.

The Balance Sheet

9

The balance sheet is a listing of asset accounts on the left side and a listing of liabilities and equity on the right side. The total of all the assets (debits) on the left is equal to (balances) the total of all liabilities and equity (credits) on the right. The reason it is called a "balance" sheet is that both the sides balance.

This can be expressed as:

Assets = Liabilities + Equity

Assets (what a company has) less liabilities (what a company owes) is equity (what the company is worth).

Assets - Liabilities = Equity

The balance sheet is the essential building block from which the income statement, statement of changes in financial position (cash flow statement), and statement of retained earnings are derived.

The balance sheet describes the financial position of a

business by recording the business' assets, liabilities, and equity at a specific point in time. This point in time is the date at the top of the balance sheet. This "snapshot in time" point of view is different from the cash flow and income statements that record performance over a period of time.

Assets, liabilities, and equity are broken down into sub-categories.

Assets

An asset is anything the business owns that has monetary value. They are economic resources controlled by an entity as a result of past transactions or events, and from which future economic benefits may be obtained. In other words, an asset is anything the business owns that provides economic benefits.

Assets include cash, accounts receivable, inventory, equipment, land, buildings and intangibles, such as patents and copyrights. They are listed on the left side of the balance sheet in order of liquidity.

Assets are subdivided into current, capital, long-term and "other" assets to reflect the ease of liquidating each asset. Liquidating an asset simply means turning it into cash. For example, because government bonds can be easily and quickly converted to cash, they are more "liquid" than buildings that take longer to sell and turn into cash.

Current assets

Current assets are any assets that can be easily converted into cash (or used up in earning revenue, such as inventory that gets sold) within one calendar year. Examples of current assets would be the bank checking account, money market accounts, accounts receivable, and notes receivable that are due within one year's time.

Generally cash is presented first, and then accounts receivable, and then inventory, with other current assets fitting in between, depending on their liquidity.

Capital assets

Capital assets, also called "fixed" assets, are intended for long-term use to earn revenue. These include tangible items such as land, buildings, machinery, and vehicles.

Long-term assets

Long-term assets are assets that are not expected to be converted into cash in the short-term nor consumed in the production of income within one calendar year. An example is a long-term investment, such as a 30-year bond.

Other assets

Other assets include assets that do not fit into any of the other categories, including intangibles such as goodwill, patents, and copyrights, and deferred items (such as deferred taxes).

Liabilities

Liabilities are the claims of creditors against the assets of the business. These include all debts and obligations owed by the business to outside creditors, suppliers, or banks that are payable within one year. Examples are accounts payable, bank loans, and notes payable.

Liabilities are subdivided into current and long-term liabilities to reflect the due dates of repayment. They are listed on the right side of the balance sheet, with the terms of repayment determining the order in which they will be presented (the shorter-term debts first).

Current liabilities

Current liabilities include all debts and obligations owed by the business to outside creditors, vendors, or banks that are expected to become due within one year. Examples are trade accounts payable, accrued payroll, and notes payable falling due within the next year.

Long-term liabilities

Long-term liabilities are debts or obligations owed by the business that are expected to become due more than one year out from the balance sheet date, such as mortgages payable.

Equity

Equity is made up of two items: capital stock (shares) and retained earnings (undistributed profits).

Capital stock

Capital stock is the original price (issuance price) at

which the shares were sold to shareholders. The price at which these shares are subsequently sold is irrelevant for financial statement purposes; it is a private matter between shareholders.

Retained earnings

Retained earnings are the accumulated earnings of the corporation less dividends distributed to shareholders to date.

At least two years

The balance sheet and the rest of the financial statement components are presented with comparative numbers for at least the current and past year. Sometimes companies choose to include three years.

Having comparative figures allows the investor and lender to look for trends. For example, are sales going up or down? Are costs in line with the direction of the sales increase or decrease?

Trends

The statement of changes in financial position summarizes the changes in the assets and liabilities that have occurred during the last accounting period. Do you see a trend? Trends are important because they can help investors see potential for gains or losses. They can highlight areas that are worthy of further study. They can also point out areas that might become problem areas in the future.

When you spot a trend you need to ask yourself if

management has plans in place to take advantage of a good thing, or do they have a contingency plan to handle a storm on the horizon?

Commitments and contingencies

Commitments and contingencies are possible expenditures that may or may not have to be made depending on the outcome of specific events such as court cases and insurance settlements. These are presented by U.S. companies under the caption "Commitments and Contingencies" on the face of the balance sheet with a reference directing the reader to the appropriate note in the financial statements.

Canadian companies, although not obligated to do so, are quickly adopting the same practice, to avoid litigation, given the atmosphere created by Sarbanes-Oxley.

Making large numbers easier to read

Since many companies deal in very large sums of money, to make the financial statements easier to read they will remove the extra zeros and state that the financial statements are in thousands, or millions. For example, if the financial statements are "in thousands" $800,000 would be written as 800. If it are written "in millions" $800,000,000 would be written as 800. The notes to the financial statements will also indicate the recording currency.

On the following page is an example of a Balance Sheet.

XYZ Limited
Balance Sheet (in thousands)
December 31, 2008

Assets	2009	2008
Current assets		
Cash	800	1080
Accounts receivable	7600	4450
Due from related company	1400	1000
Inventory	8500	4780
Prepaid expenses	722	522
Other assets		
Investment in related company	3340	4200
Capital assets	24320	18650
	46682	34682
Liabilities		
Current liabilities		
Accounts payable	6050	4196
Accrued liabilities	3742	2340
Notes payable	4000	3000
Current portion of long-term debt	4500	1340
Income taxes payable	690	164
Deferred taxes-current portion	200	180
	19182	11220
Other liabilities		
Long-term debt	9500	8720
Deferred taxes	1300	1120
	29982	21060
Shareholders equity		
Capital stock		
Common	7956	5956
Preferred	4000	4000
Retained earnings	4744	3666
	16700	13622
Contingent liability	46682	34682

The Income Statement 10

The income statement is a summary of the financial transactions (revenues and expenses) for the period. The period can be for a month, 3 months (quarter), or a year. The year need not be a calendar year. It can be any 12-month period (fiscal year). Generally accepted accounting principles (GAAP) enable income statements from year to year or from different companies to be compared.

Revenue

Revenue usually means income generated from the sale of goods or the rendering of services. In addition, revenues can include rental income, interest, dividends, and royalties, just to name a few.

There is no standard way of presenting revenue on financial statements. It will vary. Small companies can have a single line for their sales, while large conglomerates can separate their consolidated (total) sales by product, division, or location.

Cost of goods sold

Cost of goods sold is the total cost of finished goods sold during the period. These goods can have been purchased or manufactured. If they were manufactured, the cost of goods manufactured includes direct materials and labor.

Gross profit

The cost of goods sold is deducted from sales to arrive at gross profit. This is how much the company made from its core operations.

Net income

If revenues exceed expenses for the period, the company earned a profit (net income). If expenses exceed revenues for the period, the company incurred a loss (net loss). When all expenses and costs are deducted from the revenue figure, it is easy to see why the resulting net income or loss is called "the bottom line."

While some new companies may not be expected to be profitable for a few years, over the long run, no company can survive without profits and positive cash flow.

Loss carry-forward and carry-back provisions

Losses can be carried forward or carried back a number of years. This lets companies restate accounting income or losses to reduce taxes.

Other income

Revenues that don't come from the core operations of the business are classified as "other income." This includes items such as capital gains (or losses) made from investments, or income from the rental of properties. Although some of this income may be received regularly, such as from yearly dividends, it is still considered other income because it is outside of the main business activities.

Extraordinary and unusual items

Income and losses that are not incurred in the "ordinary" course of a company's regular business are classified as "extraordinary." They are a result of events and transactions differentiated by their unusual nature and by the infrequency of their occurrence.

Extraordinary items are usually not a result of management decisions. For example, if a company wins a patent infringement lawsuit and receives damages, the "extraordinary" income is added to income that year. On the other hand if a loss occurs because of a natural disaster, the "extraordinary" loss is subtracted from income.

Discontinued operations

When a company sells off or discontinues a segment of its business, it reports this event in this section of the financial statement. For example, if a company decides to abandon a certain product line, it reports the effect of the closing in this section.

Expenses

Expenses are incurred when assets are being used up as a result of business activity. They are the costs of doing business excluding cost of goods sold. Some examples of expenses are wages and salaries, advertising and promotion, legal and accounting fees, rent, insurance, telephone, heat, light, power, etc.

General operating expenses

General operating expenses include items such as marketing, salaries, insurance, office rent, etc. Any normal expense incurred in the day-to-day operations of the company falls under this category.

Depreciation

Depreciation is the recording of the expense of using up an asset. For example if a company bought a piece of machinery that cost $10,000, which is expected to last 10 years, the depreciation expense would be $1000 per year.

Because depreciation represents the reduction in the useful life span of an asset, it is important for investors to understand that depreciation is a "non-cash" expense. In other words, depreciation is an accounting entry that reduces only accounting income, but not cash. Cash will be a consideration only when it is time to replace the particular asset with a new one.

This point is critical for lenders and suppliers who extend credit to companies. When lenders analyze financial statements, they are trying to determine if there is a good chance they will be repaid. Companies do not pay their bills with accounting profits. They pay their debts with cash.

EBITDA

EBITDA is an acronym that means "earnings before interest, taxes, depreciation, and amortization." It is often used as a benchmark to judge company performance before taking into account the cost of borrowing and government taxes.

Interest

Interest is the cost of borrowing form external sources, such as banks. This is not to be confused with the cost of capital.

Cost of capital

The cost of capital is the rate of return that investors would receive if they invested their money someplace else with similar risk. If the company does not at least earn this rate of return, investors will start thinking about moving their money out of the company to where it can earn a better return. Many companies use the minimum required rate of return to decide if a project is worth doing, such as introducing a new product, with its anticipated return on investment.

Income taxes

Income taxes include federal, state, provincial, and municipal income taxes, but do not include other taxes such as duty and import taxes. Only a corporation records income tax expense. Other forms of business let the profits flow to the business owners as personal income.

Tax laws often permit a deferral of corporate income taxes, which can add up to substantial savings for the company. Many companies are acquired for their tax deferral, which can be applied to the purchasing company's income. Investors should pay close attention to any tax deferral account they see. It may be the sign of a company in which it is worth investing.

Earnings per share (EPS)

"Earnings per share" (EPS) is the amount of net income per share.

$$\textbf{Earnings per share} = \frac{\textbf{total earnings}}{\textbf{the total number of shares outstanding}}$$

There are only 2 ways of increasing EPS:

Increased earnings
Decrease the number of shares

Investors need to examine why the EPS has gone up. Did the actual earnings increase, or did the company buy back shares?

Timing issues

There are often timing issues when it comes to reporting revenue and expenses. For example, although an insurance premium is paid once a year, its cost is spread out over each month of the year. The monthly insurance expense is 1/12 of the premium. Another example, on the revenue side, is that credit sales are reported in the month of the sale, not in the month the money is collected.

Investors will often find clues to timing differences in the notes to the financial statements. The notes will explain the accounting policy the company uses. Changes in accounting policy will also be reported in the notes to the financial statements.

Trends

Investors need to look at more than the most current income statement. It must be compared to at least the previous year's income statement and preferably to more. Investors should look for trends such as increasing or decreasing sales and expenses. Investors need to decide if past performance is a real indicator of future performance. In other words, there should be clues about whether the company will make money in the future.

On the following page is an example of an Income Statement.

XYZ Limited
Income Statement (in thousands)
Year Ended December 31, 2008

	2007	2008
Sales	35000	31000
Cost of goods sold	21854	18900
Gross profit	13146	12100
Expenses		
Selling, general and administrative	4900	6290
Depreciation	1700	620
Interest	3150	1958
Other expenses	480	560
	10230	9428
Operating income	2916	2672
Investment income	320	540
	3236	3212
Provision for income taxes		
Current	1066	920
Deferred	200	410
	1266	1330
Net income	1970	1882

The Cash Flow Statement 11

U.S. companies tend to use the term "Cash Flow Statement" while Canadian companies call the same statement the "Statement of Changes in Financial Position."

The cash flow statement provides information about how a company finances its day-to-day operations as well as its long-term investments and asset purchases.

The cash flow statement provides investors and lenders information about a company's solvency and liquidity. The company is solvent when it can meet its obligations as they fall due. It is insolvent when it can no longer pay its bills on time.

A company's liquidity refers to how much cash it has and how fast it can convert its other assets to cash. The easier and faster the company can sell its assets to get cash, the more "liquid" it is.

The cash flow statement starts with the cash balance at the beginning of the period and ends with the cash balance at the end of the period. The change in the cash balance from the beginning of the period to the end of the period, either an increase in cash or a decrease in cash, is a result of changes in the assets, liabilities, and equity on the balance sheet during the period.

Sources of cash flow

A company will have three main sources of cash flow:

1) Operations, which refers to cash flow coming from sales.

2) Shareholder investment, which refers to cash invested in the company by shareholders.

3) Borrowing which refers to money obtained from lenders.

The sources that have already been tapped will be apparent in the statement of changes in financial position. However, there may be sources that have not yet been used. Does the company have access to additional sources of cash?

Profitable companies can go broke

I know I have stated this repeatedly throughout this book, but if there is one thing I want you to take from this, it is to never be lulled into complacency by profits.

I looked at one company that was extremely profitable whose sales were increasing. They had a wonderful record with their suppliers, whose accounts were always paid on time. Upon closer examination of the statement of changes of financial position, one could see that inventory was not being turned over as fast as sales were rising, and the collection of the accounts receivable was lagging behind sales more and more.

The company was managing to pay its bills on time by borrowing long-term from the bank against the company assets. The company reached a point where there were no more free and clear assets left to pledge to the bank. The bank refused to advance any more funds.

Desperate for cash flow, the company began to drop its prices and extend credit terms, and stopped spending on required maintenance as well as vital research and development.

The bank could see what was happening because of the deterioration in key ratios it required be maintained as part of its financing agreement (these are known also as "covenants") with its client. The bank called the loan because it was worried that the assets it counted on as collateral (inventory, accounts receivable, equipment, and buildings) would deteriorate and the bank would not be able to sell these assets for enough to get paid in full. The company eventually declared bankruptcy, the bank was paid, and the suppliers were left high and dry, along with the investors.

On the following page is an example of a Cash Flow Statement.

XYZ Limited
Cash Flow Statement (in thousands)
December 31, 2008

Operating activities	2007	2008
Net income	1970	1882
Depreciation	1700	620
Deferred income taxes	200	410
	3870	2912
Working capital		
Accounts receivable	(3150)	(2390)
Due from company	(400)	(270)
Inventory	(3720)	(66)
Prepaid expenses	(200)	(142)
Notes payable	1000	3000
Accounts payable	1854	676
Accrued liabilities	1402	350
Income taxes payable	526	(176)
Cash from operating activities	1182	3894
Investing activities		
Additions to capital assets	(7370)	(11464)
Investment in related company	860	(410)
Cash used in investing activities	(6510)	(11874)
Financing activities		
Issuance of long-term debt	3940	2700
Issuance of preferred shares	------	4000
Issuance of common shares	2000	2150
Dividends paid	(892)	(830)
Cash from financing activities	5048	8020
(Decrease) Increase in Cash	(280)	60
Cash - beginning of year	1080	1020
Cash - end of year	**800**	**1080**

Statement of Retained Earnings

12

Retained earnings are "earnings" that are "retained" by the company. They are the profits that have not been given back to the investors as dividends.

Retained earnings fuel future growth

The rate at which the company "retains" its earnings is a strong indicator of its financial health. For example, a company just starting out will retain its earnings to fuel growth. On the other hand, more mature companies tend to have a regular dividend policy in order to keep investors from moving their money to younger companies with a greater potential for a quick increase in stock price.

Dividends

If the company is not doing as well as promised in its business plan, it may be forced into issuing dividends sooner than planned in order to keep the share price up and shareholders happy.

I remember one company at the height of high-tech

boom that had a sound business plan, experienced management, and adequate startup capital. Unfortunately, it was not alone in its market. The fierce competition forced this company to forgo most of its profit and therefore had very little retained earnings.

Although a company may have excellent prospects, its lack of retained earnings is usually an indicator of low profits, strong competition, or inadequate startup capital.

Retained earnings are either used for future business projects or invested back into the company for growth purposes. It is important for investors to understand a company's policies and goals with regard to dividends and retained earnings. If investors want income, they should look for companies with a history of paying dividends. If investors are looking to increase the value of their shares, they should look for companies that reinvest profits for future growth.

On the following page is an example of a Statement of Retained Earnings.

XYZ Limited
Statement of Retained Earnings (in thousands)
Year Ended December 31, 2009

	2007	2008
Retained earnings - beginning of year	1500	1800
Net income	500	200
Dividends	(200)	(100)
Retained earnings - end of year	1800	1900

Notes to the Financial Statements 13

Following the auditor's opinions and the company's financial statements are the notes to the financial statements, sometimes called "footnotes". The notes further explain the organization's financial activities. Reading the notes carefully is fundamental to evaluating and understanding the financial statements.

People often assume that financial statement analysis is about performing mathematical calculations based on the numbers provided in the financial statements. But the truth is that a thorough analysis begins with plenty of reading long before you pull out your calculator. You might not even bother to perform any calculations if you don't like what you are reading.

Most people do not bother to read the notes to the financial statements or, if they do read them, they do not have the patience to read through all the details. But notes are an crucial part of the financial statements. The financial statements are not complete without them. In the notes, the company provides the necessary disclosures and explanations about how it prepared the financial statements, and the policies used to make accounting decisions. They often hold the key to highlighting areas that need to be examined closely. For example, significant contingent liabilities can be disclosed in the notes without showing up as debt on the balance sheet.

Reading through the notes can certainly pay off. As I pointed out at the beginning of the book, James Chanos read the notes to Enron's financial statements over and over again, but still could not understand them. He suspected something was wrong. He shorted the stock and reaped the benefits when the stock price tumbled.

Another example of the importance of reading the notes to the financial statements is a situation where a high-tech company indicated in a two-line remark that its research and development spending had dropped substantially in the past year. Its reduced cash flow that year did not allow it to keep ahead of its competition in product development. This is an alarm bell and the reader needs to question what is really going on.

Nature of the company's business

Usually the first note is a short description of the nature of the company's business. Knowledge of the particular company's business that differentiates it from the other companies in the same industry is important. Public companies that operate in more than one industry must also provide financial statements by industry, or segment. Investors, lenders should know the history of the company, its major lines of business, and the most important accounting policies used by the company.

Disclosure requirements

Whether something should be disclosed in the notes to the financial statements is a matter of professional judgment, standards set out in the generally accepted accounting standards, and statute requirements. Notes should address new problems as they come up to help meet the needs of investors, lenders, prospective buyers, and, of course, must accommodate any changes in legal reporting requirements.

Contingent liabilities

Notes to the financial statements describe the company's contingent liabilities. A "contingent" liability is a potential future obligation (or impairment of an asset, such as a lien on a building) to an outside party for an unknown amount, such as a parent company's loan guarantee for a subsidiary. For example, a pending court case against the company by a client could result in a liability, but it is difficult to predict the amount because it depends on the court's decision.

Something may be in the notes because the likelihood of the event occurring is difficult to assess. Where the company is involved in a court battle over patent rights, for example, an educated guess has to be made as to the possible outcome and possible eventual financial impact.

Other examples include pending litigation for product liability, income tax disputes, and product warranties.

Contingent liabilities disclosure guidelines

If there is only a "remote" (slight) chance of a negative

outcome and creation of a liability (or impairment of an asset), then no disclosure is necessary.

If there is a "reasonably possible" chance (more than remote, but less than probable) a negative outcome and creation of a liability (or impairment of an asset), then disclosure in the notes is necessary.

If there is a "probable" chance (likely to occur) of a negative outcome and creation of a liability (or impairment of an asset), then disclosure depends on the ease of estimating the amount of the liability (or amount of asset impairment).

If the amount can be reasonably estimated, then the financial statement accounts need to be adjusted. If the amount cannot be reasonably estimated, then disclosure in the notes is necessary. Obviously, deciding the treatment and disclosure method requires professional judgment.

Responsibility for disclosure of contingent liabilities

Management, not the auditor, is responsible for identifying and deciding the appropriate accounting treatment for contingent liabilities. Auditors usually require management's cooperation to become aware of contingent liabilities.

Contingent commitments

Closely related to contingent liabilities are contingent commitments. Some examples are commitments to purchase raw materials, lease facilities, bonus plans, and profit-sharing plans. The common characteristic of these items is the agreement to commit the firm to a set of fixed conditions (such as a contract to buy certain quantities at a fixed price in the next year), regardless of the company's performance.

Disclosure of contingent commitments

All commitments are described together in a separate note or included in the note about contingent liabilities. While the auditor has a duty to look at sales and purchase contracts, these disclosures rely on management's cooperation.

Subsequent events

The auditor must review transactions and events after the balance sheet date (and prior to the auditor's report) to see if anything happened that might change the financial statements.

Two kinds of "subsequent events" require a review by management and appraisal by the auditor:

- Those that require adjusting the numbers in the financial statements.
- Those that only need to be disclosed in the notes.

Subsequent events that change the numbers

Subsequent events that affect the numbers are the result of additional information coming to light that seriously changes the financial condition of the company. For example, a significant account receivable becomes uncollectible because of the bankruptcy of a key customer.

Subsequent events that need only disclosure

Subsequent events that do not require an adjustment of the numbers on the financial statements, but need to be disclosed in the notes are also a result of additional information coming to light, but do not have quite as serious an effect on the numbers. Examples include a decline in the value of marketable securities after year-end, a drop in the value of inventory because of new laws that prevent further sale of the product, and uninsured losses because of a fire.

Going concern

One of the generally accepted accounting principles that the auditor uses is the basic assumption that the business is a "going concern." This means that the business is being run with the intent of lasting a long time. If there is any concern about the survival of the business, the notes to the financial statements need to disclose the auditor's apprehension. For example, the business may be in a "sunset" industry where demand for the product or service is dying out, such as the manual typewriter business.

On-going concern disclosure

The auditor has a duty to judge whether there is any significant doubt about the company's ability to continue as a going-concern for at least one year beyond the balance sheet date. This may occur as a result of subsequent information being received. For example, if the auditor discovers that the company has defaulted on its major bank loan, or has lost its largest customer, the situation may dictate that the auditor note that there is concern about the company's ability to exist in the future.

Depending on the information obtained, the situation may require altering the audit opinion, adjustment of the numbers in the financial statements, or disclosure in the notes to the financial statements.

Related party transactions

Another area that deserves close scrutiny is "related party" transactions. If related party transactions are material, they should be disclosed in the financial statements. Generally accepted accounting principles require disclosure of the nature of the related party relationship and a description of transactions, including dollar amounts. The issue is not only accounting disclosure requirements, but also the lack of independence between the parties involved in the transaction. Related party notes may be the only indication that the organization may be engaged in a conflict of interest.

A related party is defined as an affiliated company, a principal owner of the company, or any other party which can influence the management or operating policies of the other. Examples of related parties include a subsidiary, an officer who receives a company loan, and another company related through common directorship.

Purchases from related parties

If the company purchases its raw materials from related parties, it may be subject to shortages because of management's unwillingness to buy elsewhere. It may be also buying at prices that are higher than if it purchased from competing suppliers.

Accounts receivable from related parties

If accounts receivable from a related party are material, then investors, lenders, and potential buyers need to pay close attention. If the credit risk of these related party accounts receivables is poor, then the possibility of not collecting them should be taken into account.

Related party remuneration

The user of the financial statements needs to look at the remuneration of related parties to make sure that it is not excessive. This includes not only large payments, but also numerous small payments that add up to significant amounts. The level of remuneration to related parties needs to approximate the going market price of similar services or products provided by unrelated parties.

Secured assets

The notes to the financial statements will give the details of assets pledged as security for loans, such as accounts receivable and inventory to secure bank lines of credit. It is important to investors, lenders, and potential buyers of the company to know the extent to which the value of the asset is pledged as collateral. If the level of debt is small compared to the value of the asset, there may be room to borrow more against that asset. This may provide emergency working capital if needed.

Using the notes to understand how many and to what extent the assets of a company are "encumbered" by collateral pledges is important. It is a gage of the amount of "wiggle room" available for additional financing.

Watch for assets that are "double pledged." In other words, look for assets that are used as collateral to one or two or more creditors. For example, the bank may use manufacturing equipment as collateral and the supplier of the equipment may also have a lien on the same equipment. This means that it is likely that only one of the creditors will be paid from the sale of this used equipment in the event of a default. It also means that the company has too much debt compared to its assets. Its only hope is to make enough profit from operations to overcome the additional debt and interest and make all the payments on time.

Secured parties

The notes to the financial statements will also indicate who holds the assets as security, and the details of the agreement such as the date, duration, and terms of repayment of the deal. In addition, readers of the financial statements should watch for assets pledged as collateral to related parties.

Significant accounting policies

Notes to the financial statements will spell out the company's significant accounting policies when the company has choices about which accounting policies to use. These include such items as policies for depreciation (long-term assets such as plants and equipment), reserves (inventory obsolescence and allowance for uncollectible accounts receivable), estimates (useful life of assets and leasehold improvements), and other measurements that require management's judgment.

Beyond the numbers

The notes to the final statements can point out areas that need further clarification. They can help readers formulate the questions that will provide a further understanding of the financial statements. In other words, the notes to the financial statements help investors and lenders to see beyond the numbers.

Reading Between the Lines 14

The things that are not on the financial statements are sometimes more important than what is there. "Reading between the lines" is an ability that comes with practice.

When you have completed your financial statement analysis, the result should be a list of questions. The answers to those questions determine how much you can trust management. Are they easy to approach? Is the information they provide clear and concise? Do they have plans in place to deal with problem areas? Or are they secretive and want to give you only the bare minimum? As an investor, management attitude is one of the most important factors in an investment decision.

Reputation

A company's reputation, especially with its customers, takes a long time to build up. It can be very valuable, but difficult, if not impossible, to measure in financial terms. However, it should be a consideration in analyzing the overall value of a company.

Market share

How much a company has of its market is an important consideration. The closer the company is to a monopoly, the more it can charge for its product and get good deals from its suppliers. The more competitive the market in which the company operates, the less chance it has to earn extra profit and get great deals from its suppliers.

Management competency/strengths/ethics

Management's ability to run the company well on a day-to-day basis will dictate whether the shareholders are getting the most out of their investment dollars and if suppliers and creditors will be paid as agreed.

In addition, management integrity sets the tone for the whole organization. Ethical behaviour must not only be encouraged, management must practise it every day. A code of ethics is not just something to talk about, but something that must actually be practiced on a daily basis.

Sarbanes-Oxley compliance

For publicly traded companies Sarbanes-Oxley compliance is not an option. If a publicly traded company is not in compliance, lenders and investors need to find out why. It could be that not enough resources have been assigned to this task, or it could be that management is trying to hide something. In both cases, it does not reflect well on management.

Unfortunately, some companies say they are SOX

compliant when they actually are not. I was asked by a large U.S. multi-national company to help with SOX compliance. They had purchased a large competitor. They claimed that they were SOX compliant because the acquired company said it was compliant. After only a few days, I discovered that the acquired company was not compliant. When I approached the auditors, they said that the division of the company I was examining was "out of scope" and that this division, with sales into the many millions of dollars was immaterial! I had to remind them that this may be a possibility in a regular audit, but when it comes to SOX compliance, the auditors are responsible for signing off on the consolidated statements, which include all divisions.

Employees - skill level/human capital

The skill level of employees is a key success factor for many companies. You will not find this in the financial statements, but talking to people who work for the company can tell you a lot. If they are happy working there and are being challenged adequately this will tell you that management is doing something right.

Political issues/currency risk

The geographic location of a company's market can present risks that are difficult to measure. For example, if a subsidiary is operating in a politically unstable country, the company's investment may be at risk. In addition, some countries limit the amount of profit a company can repatriate back to head office by imposing currency restrictions. One solution some companies use is to get insurance companies to underwrite these risks, usually at a hefty cost.

Level of diversification

If a company is diversified, it does not depend on a single product or sector for its success. For example, if a company supplies retail products, it could have several different products to provide stability of revenue, in case one particular product does not do well.

Accuracy of inventory figures

Inventory is reported at its cost, unless its market value drops below its cost. However, over time, products can become obsolete. The high-tech industry is a good example. Computers and cell phones need to be sold quickly because consumers want only the latest technology.

Are they sticking to their core competency?

If the company is doing what it does best, it tends to make good money at it. Too often companies expand into areas where they do not have the expertise to be successful. Unsuccessful expansions eventually show up on the financial statements.

I remember one company that got into trouble by moving away from their core competency. It was in the food distribution business and decided to leverage its fleet of trucks and drivers by adding to the items it offered its customers. They decided to add office supplies.

The company was very good at estimating the next week's food deliveries for a store by looking at what was missing on the shelves and replenishing these items in the following week's delivery. It was not as easy to guess the kind and quantity of office supplies that would be needed the following week. The company had many returns because of wrong guesses. It also had an oversupply of inventory that did not sell and often lacked what was in demand. It simply did not know the office supply business well enough. Wisely, the company decided to stick to what it knew well and went back to just delivering food. It quickly regained its market share and profitability.

Is it a sunset industry?

If the industry in which the company operates is in decline, then lenders and investors need to question the company's ability to sustain sales and profit levels. An example was the match manufacturing industry that has shrunk considerably due to the introduction of inexpensive disposable lighters as well as our awareness of the dangers of smoking and the resultant restriction on smoking in restaurants, bars, and public places.

Are they contemplating any M&A's?

Is the company being bought out? Is it considering making a significant acquisition? Companies attempt to keep this type of information secret until they are ready to make a formal statement, but news often leaks out. Rumors usually start for a reason. Occasionally it can be started by an unscrupulous trader who wants to buy or sell shares at a profit. However, most of the time, they are based on some truth. It does not mean that the company will go ahead, but you have to ask yourself what effect this event would have on your financial decision making if the rumors turn out to be accurate.

Do all the parts fit? Sustainability of performance?

Sustainability

Are the level of sales sustainable? Is there a steady record of increasing sales, or is this just a lucky year?

Level of research and development

The future of some companies, such as pharmaceuticals, depends on a significant investment in research and development. They must continually be looking for their next product or process. Look for a drop in research and development. It could be because there has been a decision to put the money into something more urgent, like paying the bills.

The sniff test

Finally, as a forensic accountant once said to me ,"After you have done all your analysis, even if the numbers all look right, if it smells bad trust your intuition, something is probably wrong."

Tools and Ratios 15

There are many ratios that can be used to evaluate companies. Everyone has their own favorites. Ratios fall into 3 main groups: profitability ratios, efficiency ratios, and solvency ratios

Analyzing ratios can be particularly valuable when choosing among companies, for example, how profitable is one company compared to another company, or to the industry average.

The following illustrations, which show how to calculate each ratio, are done using the information supplied in the financial statements from the fictitious company XYZ Limited, which is Practice Case #1 in Chapter 18 of this book.

Profitability ratios

Profitability ratios measure how well the company is doing on its investment. In other words, these ratios reflect how much profit it is making on sales, and how much return is being earned on its investment in assets.

Return on Sales (Profit Margin) (%)
= Net income after taxes/Net sales X 100

XYZ Return on sales = 1970/35,000 = 5.6%

This ratio measures how much profit the company makes on each sale. The higher the percentage, the more room the company has for surviving a drop in sales. For example, a company that makes 10% profit per item sold is less vulnerable than its competitor that only makes 5% profit per item sold. A higher return on sales gives a company a greater ability to survive a price war, or a downturn in the economy.

The return on sales varies according to the industry and the number of competitors in the market. For example the oil and gas industry tends to have a higher return on sales (15-20%) while the wholesale food industry is much lower (1-2%).

Return on Assets (%)
= Net income after taxes/Total assets X 100

XYZ Return on Assets = 1970/46,682 = 4.2%

This ratio measures the amount of money the company earns on each dollar it has invested in assets.

This illustrates the return on investment that a company is earning (opportunity cost). For example, if a company was earning a 1% return on assets but could sell off those assets and earn a 3% return by investing that same money in a GIC why bother running the business.

Return on Net Worth (return on equity) (%)
= Net income after taxes/Net worth X 100

XYZ Return on Net Worth = 1970/16,700 = 11.8%

The "Return on Net Worth (Return on Equity)" ratio measures the amount of money that a company earns for every dollar tied up in equity. Like the previous "Return on Assets" ratio, this is another way of illustrating the return on investment that a company is generating.

To an investor a return of 10% or greater is acceptable depending on what other possible investment choices are available. If the return is too low investors will pull their money out and go elsewhere. Company's will often declare and pay dividends to increase the return on equity to entice investors.

However, a return that is too high in comparison to other companies in its industry is suspicious, and its sustainability is questionable.

Number of Times Interest Is Earned
= Net income before interest and tax/Annual interest expense

XYZ = (1970 + 3150 + 1066)/3150 = 1.96 times

This ratio measures how well the sales cover the cost of borrowing money to run the business. In other words it measures the relationship between the level of sales and the cost of borrowing. It indicates how leveraged the company is, how dependent they are on debt financing.

Generally .5 - 1.0 is about average. In this case the

number is quite high 1.96 which reflects a high level of debt and high interest rates on that debt in relation to its sales.

Gross Margin (%)
= Gross profit/Net sales X 100

XYZ Gross Margin = 13146/35,000 = 37.6%

This ratio measures profit before expenses. It measures how much of each sale (after paying for the product or service) is left over to pay overhead expenses and contribute to profit. The higher the gross margin percentage the better.

In this example, with a Gross Margin of 37.6%, for every $100 in sales the company would have $37.60 available to pay overhead and contribute to profit.

Efficiency ratios

Efficiency ratios measure how well a company does with the assets it has. In other words, these ratios measure the rate of return that is earned from each dollar invested in assets.

Accounts Receivable Turnover
= Accounts receivable/Net Sales

XYZ Accounts Receivable Turnover = 35,000 /7600= 4.6 times

This ratio measures how many times the accounts receivable have rolled over in the past year. This is important because the higher the turnover, the less time the company has its money tied up in accounts receivable.

In XYZ's case, the accounts receivable roll over 4.6 times in a year, which is slow. Ideally, it should be somewhere between 7-8 times. XYZ does not collect its receivables fast enough and therefore has too much money invested in its accounts receivable.

Days of Sales Outstanding (DSO) = Accounts Receivable/(Sales/365)

XYZ Days of sales outstanding =7600/(35,000/365) = 79.3 days

This ratio measures how many days of sales are invested in accounts receivable. This is significant because it shows how long a company has its money tied up instead of being available to pay its bills.

In XYZ's case, the company sells an average of $96,000 per day, and there are 79.3 of these days invested in accounts receivable. This is too high. The average for XYZ's industry is around 45 days.

Inventory Turnover = Cost of goods sold/Inventory

XYZ Cost of goods sold to inventory turnover = 21,854/8500= 2.6 times

This ratio measures how many times inventory (at cost) rolled over in the past year. This is important because the higher the turnover, the less time the company has its money tied up in inventory.

In XYZ's case, the inventory at cost rolls over 2.6 times in a year, which is very slow. Ideally, it should be somewhere between 7-8 times. XYZ does not sell its inventory fast enough and therefore has too much money invested in it. This is particularly dangerous in the computer industry because of the risk that the inventory will become obsolete.

Assets to Net Sales (%)
= Total Assets/Net sales X 100

XYZ Assets to net sales = 46,682/35,000 = 133.4%

This ratio measures the company's ability to generate sales per dollar of investment in assets. A low ratio means that the company does not need to tie up as much money in assets to generate the same amount of sales.

A company that can generate $1,000,000 worth of sales with only $500,000 invested in assets (50%) is more efficient than a company the generates the same $1,000,000 worth of sales with $1,000,000 invested in assets (100%).

In XYZ's case, 133.4% is high compared to the average for the industry which is between 75-100%.

Sales to Net Working Capital
= Net sales/Net working capital

XYZ Sales to net working capital = 35,000/((800+7600+1400+8500+722) - 19,182) = - 218.8 times

This ratio measures the relationship between sales

and working capital. Working capital is the difference between current assets and current liabilities that the company uses to pay its bills.

In XYZ's case, working capital is actually negative and therefore produces a negative sales to net working capital ratio. In healthy companies, ones with positive working capital, this ratio will reflect how well the company can generate sales for every dollar of working capital. The higher the ratio, the more efficiently the company uses its working capital, and the less likely it is that they will need to borrow any additional cash.

Accounts Payable to Sales (%)
= Accounts Payable/Net sales X 100

XYZ Accounts payable to sales = 6050/35,000 = 17.3 %

This formula measures the relationship between accounts payable and sales. It illustrates how much of the sales will have to be used to pay the bills.

In XYZ's case, the percentage of accounts payable to sales is 17.3% or $17.30 for every $100 of sales. This is high compared to the industry's average of 8%. The lower the percentage of accounts payable to sales the more money there is available from those sales to pay the bills.

Obviously, a company with a lower accounts payable to sales percentage is more efficient in the use of its resources than a company with a higher percentage. This can be critical in a downturn.

Solvency ratios

Solvency ratios measure a company's ability to meet its financial obligations as they fall due. They measure a company's ability to convert assets to cash.

Ratios for loan covenants

Loan covenants are conditions that a lender imposes on a borrower. For example, the bank may insist that the ratio of debt to equity never surpass 2 to 1. This means that the company cannot finance more than 2/3 of its needs by borrowing. The bank does this to ensure the company does not over extend itself and will have plenty of money to pay back the bank loan. This puts a lot of pressure on the company to produce financial statements that show that the company is meeting this condition. Otherwise, the bank could call the loan.

Ratios for loan covenants can be anything that the lender chooses to include in the loan documentation, but usually they are solvency ratios, since obviously the banks first concern is whether the company has the cash to make its payments.

The most common ratios used as loan covenants include debt to equity, and current assets to current liabilities.

If all things are going well, investors will not know the details of any loan covenants. The only time that these are made public knowledge is in the case of an audited financial statement when a company is in breach of the loan covenants. The auditor must make mention of any breach of covenants in the notes to the financial statements because such a breach brings into question whether the company is a going-concern.

Profit vs. cash flow

Does the company make money consistently? Profit (or loss) is the difference between revenues (the money coming in) and expenses (the money going out). Revenues and expenses are recorded on an accrual basis. This means that they are recorded when they are incurred, not when the cash is received or paid. For example, credit sales are recorded when the goods are delivered or when the services are rendered. Accounts payable are recorded as the debt is incurred, not when the bill is finally paid.

Because accrual based accounting is used, accounting profit can be recorded even though no cash has changed hands. For example, the sale of an item on credit records a sale, with an increase in accounts receivable. If the sale is profitable, then gross profit is recognized.

Measuring a company's ability to pay its bills

The difference between accounting profit and cash flow is critical because companies pay their bills with cash, not accounting profit. Investors may choose to look at the accounting net income of a company, but suppliers and lenders need to look at expected future cash flow to determine the probability of getting paid in full on time. The following solvency ratios help to determine if a company has enough cash to pay its bills on time.

Current ratio
= Total current assets/Total current liabilities

XYZ Current ratio = (800+ 7600+1400+8500+722)/19,182 = .992

The "Current Ratio" measures the company's working capital, and the relationship between assets that will be converted to cash in the short-term and the liabilities that will need to be paid in the same time frame. The more current assets a company has in relation to its current liabilities the greater its ability to produce the cash required to meet its obligations.

In this example the current ratio is .992. The ideal would be 2.0 for a company of this size. The larger the company the lower the ratio can be and still be considered to have sufficient cash.

Quick ratio
= (Cash + Accounts receivable)/ Total current liabilities

XYZ Quick Ratio = (800+7600)/19182 = .437

Because this measures the cash on hand and the Accounts Receivable (which are probably due to come in within 60 days) divided by the current liabilities this ratio measures the amount of money that a company can pull in quickly. This is often nicknamed "The Acid Test" because it is a measurement of what the company can pull in fast, in a critical situation.

Ideally you are looking for a number of 1 or greater because this indicates that the company only needs to collect its receivables in order to pay its bills and does not need to depend on converting other current assets to cash quickly. In this example, XYZ's quick ratio is less than 1. At .437 this means that in addition to collecting the outstanding receivables they must also make additional sales quickly (or somehow borrow additional funds) in order to pay their bills.

The quick ratio is often used as a lending covenant, in other words, banks will often have a clause in their loan agreements that stipulates that the company must maintain a quick ratio of 1:1 or greater. If the quick ratio falls below 1 they will call the loan. They do this to ensure that they get paid.

Total liabilities to net worth (%)
= Total liabilities/Net worth X 100

XYZ Total liabilities to net worth = 29,982/16,700 = 179.5%

This ratio is very simple. It measures how much debt (from any source) the company has in relation to its net worth.

In this example, 179.5% means that for every $100 of net worth the company has $179 of debt which makes it more vulnerable to missing a payment to lenders. Ideally you would want total liabilities to net worth to be 100% or less.

Current liabilities to net worth (%)
= Total current liabilities/Net worth X 100

XYZ Current liabilities to net worth = 19,182/16,700 = 119.7%

This ratio is different from the previous one only in its time frame, in that it uses current liabilities rather than total liabilities. This is significant because it measures the relationship between debt that must be paid currently and net worth. The greater the current liabilities in relation to net worth, the greater the likelihood that additional money will be required to cover a shortfall.

In this example, XYZ's current liabilities to net worth of 119.7% is lower than the previous calculation of total liabilities to net worth of 179.5% which shows that their vulnerablility lies more in the long term than in the short term.

Ideally you would want current liabilities to net worth to be between 50-100% or less.

Debt to equity
= Notes payable + current and long-term debt/Net worth

XYZ Debt to equity = (4,000+25,182)/16,700 = 174.7%

Debt to equity ratio is the common covenant ratio used by banks and other lenders in their loan documentation. This is similar to the total liabilities to net worth calculation. The difference is that the lender will define the categories of debt and equity that are to be included in the loan covenant.

Fixed assets to net worth (equity)(%)
= Fixed assets/Net worth X 100

XYZ Fixed assets to net worth 24,320/16,700 = 145.6%

This measures the relationship between the amount the company has invested in long-term assets and net worth. This is significant because it shows how much of the net worth is invested in permanent assets. Having too much invested in fixed assets compared to current assets means that cash flows may not accrue quickly enough to pay the bills.

In this example XYZ has fixed assets to net worth of 145.6%. The ideal would be 100%. XYZ has too much of its net worth invested in fixed assets and not enough in current assets which would provide cash flow more quickly.

Morley's Quick Method

16

Calculating the cash cycle

After spending over 25 years in the credit departments of companies, primarily manufacturing companies with very large volume/large dollar amount accounts I have done my share of analyzing financial statements. Even with large staffs and a certain amount of automation it can be a time consuming proposition. Over the years I have come to the conclusion that the fastest and easiest way of determining if a company has enough cash to pay its bills is to calculate the cash cycle.

The cash cycle is the number of days from the time the company first invests its money in inventory or in the providing of services, sells and bills the items or services to its customers (accounts receivable), collects the money from them, and has cash available again to pay for the inventory it bought or services it paid for in the first place (accounts payable).

Not only is a company's cash cycle a valuable indicator of a company's ability to pay its obligations to lenders as they fall due, but it also measures the company's capacity to take advantage of opportunities which may provide a greater return for investors.

By teaching my staff to use a consistant method I knew that if two analysts were to work with the same data I could be assured that they would arrive at similar conclusions.

This same method is appropriate for investors as well as lenders because these few simple steps tell you a great deal about a company and its management.

Here is the simple method that I have taught my staff for years. They dubbed it Morley's Quick Method and the name has stuck.

Morley's Quick Method

Accounts Receivable Days: This formula determines how long the company has it cash invested in Receivables.
Current year's sales/365 = 1 Day of sales
Current year's ending AR balance/1 Day of sales = AR Days

Inventory Days: This formula determines how long the company has it cash invested in Inventory.
Current year's sales/365 = 1 Day of sales
Current year's ending Inventory balance/1 Day of sales = Inventory Days

Cash Days Required: This formula determines how long before the company recovers the cash that it has invested in Inventory and Receivables.
Accounts Receivable Days+Inventory Days = Cash Days required

Actual Cash Days: This formula determines how long the cash on hand will last.
Current year's ending Cash balance/1 day of sales = Actual Cash Days

Accounts Payable Days: This formula determines how long the company takes to pay its bills.
Current year's sales/365 = 1 Day of sales
Current year's ending Accounts Payable balance/1 Day of sales = Accounts Payable Days

Let me walk you through an example. Let's assume that a company had sales of $730,000 last year, its accounts receivable balance was $80,000, its inventory balance is $40,000, its accounts payable balance is $120,000, and its cash balance is $20,000.

Here's how we would calculate the cash cycle:

Step 1: Calculate 1 day of sales
Sales/365 = 1 day of sales
$730,000/365 = $2,000 sold per day (1 day of sales)

Step 2: Calculate accounts receivable days
Accounts receivable/ 1 day of sales= AR days
$80,000/$2,000 per day = 40 days

Step 3: Calculate inventory days
Inventory/1 day of sales= inventory days
$40,000/$2,000 per day = 20 days

Step 4: Calculate accounts payable days
Accounts payable/1 day of sales= accounts payable days
$120,000/$2,000 per day = 60 days

Step 5: Calculate cash days
Cash/1 day of sales= cash days
$20,000/$2,000 per day = 10 days

Step 6: Calculate cash cycle days

Inventory days:	20
Accounts receivable days:	40
	60
Less: Accounts payable days	(60)
Cash cycle days	**0**

This example with **0 cash cycle days** is a perfect scenario where the company recovers the money it has invested in accounts receivable and inventory without having to borrow or dip into its cash reserve. However, most companies are less than perfect. It is extremely rare to find this situation in real life and the real skill for investors and lenders is to figure out the extent to which the company depends on borrowing or additional investment from shareholders to survive.

Positive cash cycle days represent a shortfall where the company has to pay their bills before they collect the money owed to them. This is the most common scenario.

Negative cash cycle days mean that the company collects its cash before it has to pay it out. This is a very rare situation.

As I keep repeating, even profitable companies can go broke, but we can use cash cycle analysis to determine if a company has enough cash to meet its commitments. An unprofitable company that has enough cash to stay afloat has time to overcome other problems and become profitable, but a company that can't pay its bills will soon be out of business.

Calculating the other ratios in the previous chapter can help to confirm any suspicions the lender or investor have about the company's prospects for the future.

Setting credit limits

There is no magic formula for setting a credit limit. It is a combination of the customer's needs, their credit rating, terms of sale, the competitiveness of the market, whether the goods can be returned and resold to another customer, the type of collateral, and how badly you need the business.

Setting credit limits is a huge topic that could easily fill another book, but for the purposes of this book the thing to understand is the importance of setting limits that are realistic for the customer and profitable for your company.

The credit limit should be set on the basis of the customer's cash flow, not based on accounting profits. Many companies are profitable, but have little cash flow to pay the bills. This is especially true of new companies or companies experiencing rapid growth. Sales people often advocate for the customer because their commissions are based on sales, but nothing is more detrimental to a business relationship than creating expectations that cannot be met.

Common Scenarios

17

This chapter outlines the types of situations that you might discover as a result of your analysis of a company's financial statements.

Borrowing long-term to meet short-term commitments

The bills are getting paid but where is the money coming from? When accounts receivable and inventory have not yet turned over by the time accounts payable become due, yet accounts payable are paid within agreed terms (this sometimes can be confirmed by suppliers who report that their account is being paid on time), where is the money coming from? The company might be taking out long term loans to meet short-term commitments. This works for a while until they run out of borrowing room.

One way to solve a cash flow problem is to have shareholders inject more cash into the business by purchasing additional shares. However, although the purchase of shares is deemed to be a permanent investment, it often is only a temporary solution and the cash eventually runs out again. Investors are often reluctant to inject more cash unless they can be convinced that they are not throwing good money after bad. Management will have to come up with a plan that is very compelling. Investors will almost always want to be assured that this is the last time they'll have to pull more money out of their pocket to save the company.

The other way to get cash is a much more common occurrence. The company borrows more, usually on a long-term basis. This can be in the form of bonds or bank loans. This can lead to disaster if the company does not correct the situation by realigning accounts receivable and inventory's ability to produce cash fast enough to pay accounts payable on time. It is like borrowing against your credit card to make the minimum payments on that card. Soon, you will have reached your credit limit and cannot borrow any more on that card. You will have to stop paying your bills. In a similar fashion, this is what happens when the company can no longer borrow because it has reached its "credit limit" because all its assets have been pledged as collateral against these loans.

When the company cannot pay its bills, cannot borrow, and shareholders refuse to rescue it by injecting more cash, bankruptcy is usually not far behind. This company may look good for the moment, but when it runs out of cash, it will usually be too late for lenders and investors to escape without a loss.

The evidence on the financial statements for making this determination are accounts receivable, inventory, accounts payable, and sales. If the total number of days the company has its money invested in accounts receivable (accounts receivable/(sales/365) and in inventory (inventory/(sales/365) exceeds the number of days it takes to pay its accounts payable (accounts payable/(sales/365), then look for an increase in long-term borrowing (bank loans going up) to confirm your suspicion.

To make this determination you will need the full set of comparative numbers for the current and previous years. You will need the balance sheet, income statement, statement of changes in financial position (cash flow statement), and the accompanying notes.

Enough cash flow from operations

If accounts receivable and inventory have turned over by the time accounts payable become due, then enough cash is available from operations to pay accounts payable within agreed terms (this too sometimes can be confirmed by suppliers who report that their account is being paid on time). This company is making sure that the inventory it buys has been sold and the account receivable collected before the bills for the purchase becomes due. The cash flow statement and the notes reveal no significant increases in long-term borrowing nor any significant increase in share capital.

If the total number of days the company has its money invested in accounts receivable (accounts receivable/(sales/365) and in inventory (inventory/(sales/365) is equal or below the number of days it takes to pay its accounts payable (accounts payable/(sales/365), then no significant increase in long-term borrowing (bank loans going up) will confirm that this company is a good prospect for both lenders and investors.

Profitable company with little retained earnings

A company's financial statements can show that the company is profitable and that it has sufficient cash flow for its needs. It has great prospects for maintaining these levels of cash and profit. However, the owners, through the Board's declaration and payment of dividends, can withdraw cash. Dividends are the return of company profits to the shareholders.

Financial statements will show dividends being paid and retained earnings at a relatively low level. Compare the amount of net income on the income statement to the amount of dividends paid on the statement of retained earnings. If the net income is paid out in dividends, then this is a risky company for lenders and investors because the shareholders have little to lose since they already have gotten their money back through dividends.

Retail companies

Some of the ways retail companies can get into trouble include sales falling off, inventory taking too long to turnover, unusual seasonal ups and downs, the purchase price increasing for the items they sell, and their competition deciding to set up shop next door.

The thing to watch for on the financial statements is not only for a drop in sales, but that the profit margins are dropping due to increased competition or due to an increased cost of goods. If sales have dropped, cash will suffer as well and you should watch for an increase in accounts payable. Low gross profit on the income statement coupled with increased accounts payable on the balance sheet can mean the company is reducing the selling price to get sales. If the issue is temporary, such as a seasonal dip, and the company has done well through these cycles before, then the risk is usually limited. However, if the issue is increased competition and the drop in margins is more permanent, then lenders and investors need to see this as a higher risk company.

Good company with inexperienced management

This company has the potential to do well, but seems to be underperforming. The financial statements show that the profit margins are not as high as their competitors. Their product availability is not what is should be because they cannot anticipate what will sell, and therefore do not have the inventory that would otherwise sell. They do not pay as much attention to their accounts receivable as they should and consequently the cash is slow to come in. Accounts payable are higher because they do not have the experience to drive the same bargains that their competitors are getting.

Look for accounts payable and accounts receivable on the balance sheet increasing at a greater rate than the increase in sales. This could be a good company to lend to or invest in if management learns quickly enough or if new, more experienced management is put in place or comes in as a result of an acquisition by a competitor.

Not enough cash flow and can't borrow long term

New companies at first may find that accounts receivable and inventory are too slow to pay the accounts payable on time and have no track record to get long-term borrowing in place.

These companies can be risky if they do not have sufficient cash to see them through until they develop the ability to collect their accounts quickly and buy the right inventory at the right price in the right amount.

The financial statements will often show that they are forced to stretch their accounts payable until accounts receivable and inventory provide better cash flow and that their track record will allow them to get breathing room in terms of a bank or other type of loan. If the total number of days the company has its money invested in accounts receivable (accounts receivable/(sales/365) and in inventory (inventory/(sales/365) is equal or greater to the number of days it takes to pay its accounts payable (accounts payable/(sales/365), and there is no significant increase in long-term borrowing (bank loans going up), these companies have no alternative but to get the shareholders to put more money in until things turn around.

This type of company is high risk until things settle down.

Cash rich but not profitable

If a new company has a large amount of cash to start, it should be able to weather the pains of starting up the business. However, large amounts of cash are no guarantee that lenders and investors will be paid. The financial statements may not show any revenue or profit for some time.

If the cash balances are declining and expenses are continuing to pile up faster than the increase in sales, this company is very risky if it does not have access to investors ready and able to invest more cash.

In one situation I reviewed the financial statements of a company that had over $750 million in cash. I turned down this opportunity to extend credit because the financial statements also showed that cash was declining at a rate of about $600,000 a month. They were in the business of developing sophisticated computers for the U.S. military. It required so much costly research that they ran out of money before they could produce or sell the first one.

Your investing and lending decisions should not be based solely on the level of cash the company is showing you.

High profits - low cash

If a company's financial statements show a lot of profit, and relatively low levels of cash, you should look to see if there have been increases in the level of accounts receivable. They may have made the sale, but not yet collected. You may have to ask the company what are its usual terms of sales and if there have been any unusually high sales with extended terms.

If yes, then the company may have accepted the higher risk of that sale associated with the longer terms to get the sale. Look for accounts receivable increasing faster than sales along with an increase in accounts payable. The higher profit on the sale may later disappear as a write-off of accounts receivable that cannot be collected.

Part 3
Practice Cases

For the following practice cases, determine whether you would be willing to invest or lend to each of these companies. The answers follow the data in each case.

Case #1 XYZ Limited is a fictitious company in the computer industry.

Case #2 Unique Systems Inc. is a fictitious company in the printing industry.

Case #3 Celestica Inc. a well-known electronics contract manufacturer.

Case #4 Nortel Networks Inc. a well-known company in the electronics industry

Case #5 WalMart Stores, Inc. the world's largest consumer goods retailer.

NOTE: Keep in mind that for these illustration purposes we are working with 2006 financial statements, which do not represent the current financial state of the companies.

The purpose of these practice cases is to teach you how to analyze financial statements, not to make investing or lending recommendations about particular companies.

Practice Case #1 XYZ

18

For this practice case we are using the made up financial statements of a fictitious privately held company in the computer industry.

Analyze these financial statements and determine whether or not you would be willing to lend to or invest in this company.

XYZ Limited (fictitious company)
Auditors Report

To the shareholders of XYZ Limited

We have audited the balance sheet of XYZ Limited as at December 31, 2006 and the statements of income and changes in financial position for a year then ended. These financial statements are the responsibility of the company's management. Our responsibility is to express an opinion on these financial statements based on our audit.

We conducted our audit in accordance with generally accepted auditing standards. Those standards require that we plan and perform an audit to obtain reasonable assurance whether the financial statements are free of material misstatements. An audit includes examining, on a test basis, evidence supporting the amounts and disclosures in the financial statements. An audit also includes assessing the accounting principles used and significant estimates made by management, as well as evaluating the overall financial statement presentation.

In our opinion, these financial statements presented fairly, in all material respects, the financial position of the company as at December 31, 2006 and the results of its operations for the year then ended in accordance with generally accepted accounting principles.

Toronto, Ontario
February 15, 2007

XYZ Limited (fictitious company)
Balance Sheet (in thousands)
December 31, 2006

Assets	2006	2005
Current assets		
Cash	800	1080
Accounts receivable (note 6)	7600	4450
Due from related company	1400	1000
Inventory (note 4)	8500	4780
Prepaid expenses	722	522
Other assets		
Investment in related company	3340	4200
Capital assets (notes 5 and 7)	24320	18650
	46682	34682
Liabilities		
Current liabilities		
Accounts payable	6050	4196
Accrued liabilities	3742	2340
Notes payable	4000	3000
Current portion of long-term debt (note 7)	4500	1340
Income taxes payable	690	164
Deferred taxes-current portion	200	180
	19182	11220
Other liabilities		
Long-term debt (note 7)	9500	8720
Deferred taxes	1300	1120
	29982	21060
Shareholders equity		
Capital Stock (note 8)		
Common	7956	5956
Preferred	4000	4000
Retained earnings	4744	3666
	16700	13622
Contingent liability (note 3)	46682	34682

XYZ Limited (fictitious company)
Income Statement (in thousands)
Year Ended December 31, 2006

	2006	2005
Sales	35000	31000
Cost of goods sold	21854	18900
Gross profit	13146	12100
Expenses		
Selling, general & admin exp (note 11)	4900	6290
Depreciation	1700	620
Interest	3150	1958
Other expenses	480	560
	10230	9428
Operating income	2916	2672
Investment income	320	540
	3236	3212
Provision for income taxes (note 9)		
Current	1066	920
Deferred	200	410
	1266	1330
Net income	1970	1882
Retained earnings - beginning of year	3666	2614
Dividends	(892)	(830)
	4744	3666

XYZ Limited (fictitious company)
Statement of Changes in Financial Position
December 31, 2006

	2006	2005
Operating activities		
Net income	1970	1882
Depreciation	1700	620
Deferred income taxes	200	410
	3870	2912
Working capital		
Accounts receivable	(3150)	(2390)
Due to related company	(400)	(270)
Inventory	(3720)	(66)
Prepaid expenses	(200)	(142)
Notes payable	1000	3000
Accounts payable	1854	676
Accrued liabilities	1402	350
Income taxes payable	526	(176)
Cash provided from operating activities	1182	3894
Investing activities		
Additions to capital assets	(7370)	(11464)
Investment in related company	860	(410)
Cash used in investing activities	(6510)	(11874)
Financing activities		
Issuance of long-term debt	3940	2700
Issuance of preferred shares	------	4000
Issuance of common shares	2000	2150
Dividends paid	(892)	(830)
Cash provided by financing activities	5048	8020
(Decrease) Increase in Cash	(280)	40
Cash - beginning of year	1080	1020
Cash - end of year	800	1080

Notes to the financial statements for the year ended December 31, 2006

1. General

XYZ Limited is an electronic contract manufacturer of products used in the high-tech computer industry.

2. Summary of Significant Accounting Policies

(a) Inventory

Inventory is valued at the lower of cost (first in, first out method) or net realizable value.

(b) Capital Assets

Property, plant and equipment are listed at their cost less accumulated depreciation. Depreciation is calculated on the estimated useful lives of the assets that range from 4 to 20 years.

(c) Investment in Related Company

The equity method of accounting is used to value the investment in common shares of a related company.

(d) Income taxes

Deferred income taxes are the tax effects of timing differences between accounting and taxable income. Investment tax credits ($265,800 in 2006 and $285,800 in 2005) were received.

(e) Product related expenses

Sales promotion expenses are recorded in the period they occur. Research and development were $244,000 in 2006 and $ 744,000 in 2005.

3. Contingent liability

During 2006, the company filed a court action against a customer for cancelling a contract and sued the customer for $1,106,734 for amounts due in damages. The customer countersued for $2,200,000. As of the date of the auditor's report, the company lawyer and management were unable to estimate the possible end result.

4. Inventory

	2006	2005
Finished goods	6400	2400
Work-in-process	900	980
Raw materials	1200	1400
	8500	4780

5. Capital assets

	2006	2005
Land	3500	2500
Buildings	15834	11352
Leasehold improvements	622	544
Machinery and equipment	8326	6612
Furniture and fixtures	1346	1250
	29628	22258
Less: accumulated depreciation	(5308)	(3608)
Net property, plant and equipment	24320	18650

6. Notes payable

As of December 31, 2006, $2,000,000 of bank short-term notes were outstanding using a general security agreement over book debts. Unused lines of credit of $250,000 were available at 2% above the prime-lending rate.

7. Long-term debt

	2006	2005
(a) 11% bond, payable 2007 to 2011	4000	-----
(b) 12% bond, payable 2008 to 2009	550	550
(c) 13% bond, payable 2005 to 2009	730	930
(d) 2006 bank term loan at 1.5% above prime, payable 2007 to 2011	1280	-----
(e) 2005 bank term loan at 1% above prime, payable 2006 to 2014	2660	3180
(f) 2004 bank term loan at 0.75% above prime, payable 2005 to 2014	4050	4470
	14000	10060
Less: Current portion	(4500)	(1340)
	9500	8720

On December 31, 2007 capital assets with net book values of about $3,700,000 and $2,100,000 have been pledged as collateral for the 11% bond and 13% note, respectively. The land and building are collateral for the bank term loans.

The loan agreements of 2006, 2005 and 2004 stipulate that the company maintain a debt-to-common-equity ratio of no more than 2.5 to 1; otherwise, they will be payable upon demand and the company may be required to apply the money from the sale of assets to prepay the loans.

Amounts of long-term debt at December 31, 2006 are:

2007	$	4500
2008		4920
2009		1240
2010		2600
2011 and later		740
		14000

8. Capital stock

Authorized:
1,000,000 common shares
1,000,000 nonvoting, non-participating preferred shares

Issued	2006		2005	
	# of shares	$	# of shares	$
Common	795,600	7956	595,600	5956
Preferred	400,000	4000	400,000	4000
		$ 11956		$ 9956

9. Income taxes

Income before income taxes	$	3236
Tax provision		1332
Decrease in taxes resulting from capital gains		(90)
Taxes for non-deductible amount		24
		633

10. Lease commitments

Annual rental commitments under IT and office equipment leases having initial or non-cancellable terms in excess of one year as at December 31, 2006 are:

2007	$	180
2008		180
2009		180
2010		80
2011		80
After 2011		120
		540

11. Related party transactions

Selling, general and administrative expenses include a technical development fee paid to a related company of $620,000 in 2006 and $540,000 in 2005.

XYZ Limited (fictitious company)- additional information from 2004 unqualified audited financial statements:

December 31, 2004

Assets	
Cash	1040
Accounts receivable	2060
Due from related company	730
Inventory	4714
Prepaid expenses	380
	8924
Investment in related company	3790
Fixed assets	7806
	20,520
Liabilities	
Accounts Payable	3520
Accrued liabilities	1990
Current portion of long-term debt	480
Income taxes payable	340
Current deferred taxes	150
	6480
Long-term debt	6880
Deferred taxes	740
	14,100
Common shares	3806
Retained earnings	2614
	6420
	20,520

December 31, 2004

Total revenue	26,680
Cost of goods sold	15,880
Expenses	8326
Tax	1064
Net income	705

Practice Case #1 Answer

Calculations

Accounts Receivable Days

Sales		$ 35,000
1 Day of sales	(35,000/365)	$ 96
Accounts receivable ending balance		$ 7600
Ending AR balance/1 Day of sales	(7600/96)	79
Accounts Receivable Days		**79 days**

Inventory Days

Sales		$ 35,000
1 Day of sales	(35,000/365)	$ 96
Inventory ending balance		$ 8500
Ending Inventory balance/1 Day of sales	(8500/96)	89
Inventory Days:		**89 days**

Accounts Payable Days

Sales		$ 35,000
1 Day of sales	(35,000/365)	$ 96
Accounts payable ending balance		$ 6050
Ending Accounts Payable/1 Day of sales	(6050/96)	63
Accounts Payable Days:		**63 days**

The cash cycle time is the number days the company takes to recover its cash. For a company that resells inventory, this begins with the day of purchase of the inventory until it is sold (inventory days) and the time it waits for its invoice to be paid (accounts receivable days).

For XYZ, cash cycle time is:

Inventory days	89
Accounts Receivable Days	<u>79</u>
Total time cash invested in inventory and accounts receivable	168
LESS	
Accounts Payable days	<u>63</u>
Shortfall	**105 days**

These numbers mean that the company is paying its bills on average in 63 days although it does not recover its cash from operations for 168 days.

The terms of purchase, although not disclosed in the financial statements or the notes, would probably be on average around 30 days, with close to 60 days being the maximum they can stretch their suppliers without being cut off.

The company has increased its long-term debt pledging all its major assets (accounts receivable, inventory, equipment) as collateral to the bank. The increase is a trend that is continuing from past years as evidenced in the series of loans outlined in Notes 6 and 7.

Its inventory is not turning over at the same rate (89 days) as its sales, which indicates that there may be a portion of the inventory that is obsolescent and difficult to sell as evidenced by the bulge in finished goods. This would also explain the need to buy updated equipment.

Accounts payable is paid (63 days) before the money from accounts receivable is collected (79 days). The accounts receivable collection period is too long.

Bank covenants have been exceeded. The requirement to prevent the loan from being called is a debt-to-common-equity ratio of no more than 2.5 to 1 (Note 7). Currently its debt-to-common-equity ratio is 3.7 (14,100/3806). The company is in breach of its agreement. The bank can call the 2006, 2005, and 2004 loans at any time, forcing the sale of the assets it holds as collateral. This would put the company out of business.

Note 2 (e) - The drop in research and development from $744,000 in 2005 to $244,000 in 2006 does not bode well for this high-tech company.

The fees paid to related parties in **Note 11** are not well explained. They require further investigation.

The contingent liability is a potential drain on cash flow.

Finally, the reason for the change in auditors noted in the audit report should be confirmed.

Profitability, efficiency, and solvency ratios

The analysis of the results of the various profitability, efficiency, and solvency ratios based on the financial statements in this practice case were done as examples on pages 115-127 in Chapter 15 of this book so I will not repeat them here.

Conclusion

Cash has decreased to 800 in 2006 from 1080 in 2005. The problem lies in the slow turnover of inventory and accounts receivable. The cash tied up in these items is not available to finance the purchase of modern equipment. The cash position will likely continue to deteriorate unless the company fixes its underlying problem with inventory and accounts receivable. Until they do they must continue to increase bank debt to keep suppliers from cutting off inventory supply shipments. However, the company does not appear to have any additional assets available as collateral to borrow further from the bank.

The prognosis is poor. It is unlikely any shareholders will want to invest any more money. The bank will likely refuse any further increases in debt financing and the company will be unable to pay its suppliers. The company will be forced into bankruptcy even though its supplier accounts are current. The bank will sell off the assets to satisfy its debt and there will be little left for other creditors.

Practice Case #2 Unique Systems 19

For this practice case we are using the made up financial statements of a fictitious privately held company in the printing industry.

Analyze these financial statements and determine whether or not you would be willing to lend to or invest in this company.

Unique Systems Inc. (fictitious company)
Auditors Report

To the shareholders of Unique Systems Inc.

We have audited the balance sheet of Unique Systems Inc. as at December 31, 2006 and the statements of income and changes in financial position for a year then ended. These financial statements are the responsibility of the company's management. Our responsibility is to express an opinion on these financial statements based on our audit.

We conducted our audit in accordance with generally accepted auditing standards. Those standards require that we plan and perform an audit to obtain reasonable assurance whether the financial statements are free of material misstatements. An audit includes examining, on a test basis, evidence supporting the amounts and disclosures in the financial statements. An audit also includes assessing the accounting principles used and significant estimates made by management, as well as evaluating the overall financial statement presentation.

In our opinion, these financial statements presented fairly, in all material respects, the financial position of the company as at December 31, 2006 and the results of its operations for the year then ended in accordance with generally accepted accounting principles.

City, State
February 15, 2007

Unique Systems Inc. (fictitious company)
Income Statement
For the Year Ended December 31, 2006

Revenues:

Graphics revenue	30,000
Printing revenue	20,000
Mailing revenue	13,000
Total revenues	**63,000**

Expenses:

Salaries	30,750
Employee benefit	1,100
Office rent	2,400
Copier rental	6,600
Utilities	400
Advertising	960
Supplies	90
Interest	100
Depreciation: Office equipment	600
Total expenses before taxes	**43,000**
Income before taxes	20,000
Income tax ($20,000 X 17%)	3,400
Net income	**16,600**

Unique Systems Inc.
Balance Sheet
December 31, 2006

Assets

Cash		13,600
Accounts Receivable		13,000
Land		20,000
Office equipment	6,000	
Less: Accumulated depreciation	600	5,400
Total assets		**52,000**

Liabilities

Accounts payable	900
Income taxes payable	500
Notes payable (short-term)	1,000
Total liabilities	**2,400**

Shareholders' Equity

Contributed capital:

Capital Stock	30,000
Contributed surplus	3,000
	33,000
Retained earnings	16,600
Total shareholders' equity	49,600
Total liabilities and shareholders' equity	**52,000**

Unique Systems Inc.
Statement of Changes in Financial Position
For the Year Ended December 31, 2006

Sources of cash
Operations

Cash revenues	50,000
Less: Cash used for expenses	44,400
Cash inflow from operations	**5,600**

Financing

Investment by owners (shares issued for cash)	33,000
Loan (note payable)	1,000
Cash inflow from financing	34,000
Total cash inflow during the year	**39,600**

Uses of cash
Investing

Purchase of office equipment	6,000
Purchase land	20,000
Cash used for investing	**26,000**
Change- Increase in cash during the year	**13,600**

Practice Case #2 Answers

Accounts Receivable Days

Sales		63,000
1 Day of sales	(63,000/365)	173
Accounts receivable ending balance		13,000
Ending AR balance/ 1 Day of sales	(13,000/173)	75
Accounts Receivable Days:		**75 days**

Inventory Days

Sales		63,000
1 Day of sales	(63,000/365)	173
Inventory ending balance		0
Ending inventory balance/ 1 Day of sales	(0/173)	0
Inventory Days		**0 days**

Accounts Payable Days

Sales		63,000
1 Day of sales	(63,000/365)	173
Accounts payable ending balance		900
Ending accounts payable/ 1 day of sales	(900/173)	5
Accounts Payable Days		**5 days**

The cash cycle time is the number days the company takes to recover its cash. For a company that resells inventory, this begins with the day of purchase of the inventory until it is sold (inventory days) and the time it waits for its invoice to be paid (accounts receivable days).

For Unique Systems, cash cycle time is:

Inventory days	0
Accounts Receivable Days	75
Total time cash invested in inventory and A/R	75
LESS:	
Accounts Payable days	5
Shortfall	**70 days**

These numbers mean that the company is paying its bills on average in 5 days although it does not recover its cash from operations for 75 days.

The first item of concern is the fact that the notes to the financial statements are missing. Notes provide vital clues about the financial condition of the company.

The terms of purchase in the printing industry would probably be on average around 30 days, with close to 60 days being the maximum they can stretch their suppliers without being cut off. The question is would be why they pay their accounts in five days. Perhaps they have a bad history and cannot obtain open terms from their suppliers.

Although the company did not increase its long-term debt, its net cash flow from operations was not sufficient to cover the purchases of land and equipment. The statement of changes in financial position tells us that investors have supplied the cash for these purchases. The question is whether the company can keep asking the investors to pour more money into the company when its operations obviously do not yield enough cash to sustain it in the long run. Because we do not have the notes to the financial statements, we are missing key information with regard to the company's debt situation. Specifically, contingent liabilities could be impairing the company's ability to borrow.

Because of the nature of its business, the company carries no inventory. We can assume that it will print stock only once it receives an order from a customer. This makes sense because of the custom nature of their product. Because all inventories are sold as produced, none is left on hand at the end of the year. This would also explain the need for the purchase of equipment in order to remain competitive in the industry.

Accounts payable is paid (5 days) before the money from accounts receivable is collected (75 days). The accounts receivable collection period is too long if the company intends to continue paying its accounts payable in five days.

We know nothing about the bank covenants. We would usually find out about these in the notes to the financial statements. We can only assume that there are no bank loans except for the $1000 loan. We will assume that bank covenants have not been exceeded.

Profitability, efficiency, and solvency ratio calculations

Although working through the cash cycle days calculations is enough to give you the answers you need regarding this company, I have included the following profitability, efficiency, and solvency ratio calculations for illustration purposes.

Return on sales (Profit Margin) (%)
= Net income after taxes/Net sales X 100
16,600/63,000 X 100 = 26.3%
This is a very good return on sales.

Return on assets (%)
= Net income after taxes/Total assets X 100
16,600/52,000 X 100 = 31.9%
This is a very good return on assets.

Return on Net Worth (return on equity) (%)
= Net income after taxes/ Net worth X 100
16,600/49,600 X 100 = 33.5%
This is a very good return on net worth.

Number of Times Interest is Earned
= Net income before interest and tax/Annual interest expense
(16,600 + 100 + 3,400)/100 = 201 times
This ratio is very good because it takes very little net income to cover interest. This is because they have very little debt.

Gross margin (%)
= Gross profit/Net sales X 100
63,000/63,000 X 100 = 100%
This means that there is no cost of goods sold (they do not buy inventory) and that all the proceeds of sales are available for expenses and profit.

Solvency ratios

Current ratio
= Total current assets/Total current liabilities
(13,600 + 13,000)/ (900 + 500 +1,000) = 11.08
This is a good ratio that reflects the company's ability to produce more cash in the short-term than it has to pay out.

Quick ratio
= (Cash + accounts receivable)/Total current liabilities
(13,600 + 13,000)/ (900 + 500 +1,000) = 11.08
In this case, it is exactly the same as the current ratio because there is neither inventory nor any other current assets.

Total liabilities to net worth (%)
= Total liabilities/Net worth X 100
2400/49,600 X 100 = 4.8%
This is a very low ratio and indicates the company gets much of its financing from equity (shareholder investment and retained earnings) rather than borrowing.

Current liabilities to Net worth (%)
= Total current liabilities/ Net worth X 100
(900 + 500 +1,000)/49,600 X 100 = 4.8%
This ratio is the same as the one above because there are no long-term liabilities.

Debt to equity
= Notes payable + current and long-term debt/ Net worth
(1,000 + 900 + 500)/49,600 = .05 to 1
This is the same again because there is no long-term debt and the notes payable are short-term only.

Fixed assets to net worth (%)
= Fixed assets/ Net worth X 100
$(20,000 + 5,400)/49,600 \times 100 = 51.2\%$
This is excellent and means that about half of the company's financing is from borrowing and the other half from equity (shareholder investment and retained earnings).

Efficiency ratios

Accounts Receivable Turnover
= Net sales/Accounts receivable
$63,000/13,000 = 4.8$
This means that accounts receivable are a little slow and they turnover almost 5 times a year as opposed to 6 times (60 days).

Days of Sales Outstanding (DSO)
= Accounts receivable/(Sales/365)
$13,000/(63,000/365) = 75.3$ days
This is a little slow for this industry. It should be more like 50-60 days.

Inventory Turnover
=Cost of goods sold/ Inventory
Zero/Zero = 0
There is no inventory. This ratio is not applicable.

Assets to Net Sales (%)
= Total assets/ Net sales X 100
$52,000/63,000 \times 100 = 82.5\%$
This means that the company uses a lot of assets to produce its sales.

Sales to the Net Working Capital
= Net sales/Net working capital
63,000/(13,600 + 13,000) - (900 + 500 + 1,000) = 2.6
This is another measure of the company's efficiency in producing sales. There is $2.6 in sales for every $1 in working capital. This is a relatively low number which indicates that they are not very efficient at producing sales given their level of working capital.

Accounts Payable to Sales (%)
= Accounts payable/ Net sales X 100
900/63,000 X 100 = 1.4%
This is a measure of a company's efficiency in producing sales. In this case, while they are not very efficient at producing sales, this ratio shows that their payables are relatively low which is because they provide services rather than sell goods.

Conclusion

Cash has increased by $13,600. The problem lies in the slow turnover of accounts receivable. The cash tied up in these items is not available to finance the purchase of modern equipment. The cash position will likely require the infusion of cash by investors unless the company fixes its underlying problem with accounts receivable. Until they do they must continue to ask for more money from the investors or, alternatively, start borrowing to keep paying suppliers in five days.

We do not have information about why they have not opened 30 day accounts with suppliers. They may have been cut off from inventory supply shipments in the past. Unfortunately, the company does not appear to have any additional assets available as collateral to borrow from the bank.

The prognosis is still unclear. It is possible that shareholders may not want to invest any more money. The bank will likely want collateral in order to provide debt financing. The cheaper solution would be to use supplier financing by setting up net 30 and net 60 day accounts.

Finally, the company needs to close the gap between the 75 day collection period for its accounts receivable and the five day payment period for its accounts payable.

Practice Case #3 Celestica

20

For this practice case we are using the actual financial statements of a publicly traded company.

Celestica Inc. is a well known electronics contract manufacturer with offices and manufacturing facilities around the world. Because this is a Canadian company these financial statements are publicly available through **www.sedar.com.** but since they are also have a U.S. presence and are listed on the NYSE their financial statements are also available on **www.edgar.com.** There might be some minor differences between these financial statements due to the differences between U.S. and Canadian GAAP, differences that the new International Financial Reporting Standards with soon do away with.

The notes to the financial statements are too large to be included in this book, but they too can be read on-line at www.sedar.com.

Keep in mind, that for these illustration purposes we are working with 2006 financial statements, which do not represent the current financial state of the company.

Celestica Inc.
Auditors Report

Auditors' Report to the Shareholders

We have audited the consolidated balance sheets of Celestica Inc. as at December 31, 2006 and 2005 and the consolidated statements of operations, shareholders' equity and cash flows for each of the years in the three-year period ended December 31, 2006. These financial statements are the responsibility of the Company's management. Our responsibility is to express an opinion on these financial statements based on our audits.

We conducted our audits in accordance with Canadian generally accepted auditing standards. Those standards require that we plan and perform an audit to obtain reasonable assurance whether the financial statements are free of material misstatement. An audit includes examining, on a test basis, evidence supporting the amounts and disclosures in the financial statements. An audit also includes assessing the accounting principles used and significant estimates made by management, as well as evaluating the overall financialstatement presentation. In our opinion, these consolidated financial statements present fairly, in all material respects, the financial position of the Company as at December 31, 2006 and 2005 and the results of its operations and its cash flows for each of the years in the three-year period ended December 31, 2006 in accordance with Canadian generally accepted accounting principles.

KPMG LLP
Chartered Accountants
Toronto, Canada
February 14, 2007

CELESTICA INC.
CONSOLIDATED BALANCE SHEETS
(In millions of U.S. dollars)
Year ended December 31, 2006

Assets	2005	2006
Current assets:		
Cash and short-term investments	969.0	803.7
Accounts receivable	982.6	973.2
Inventories	1,058.4	1,197.9
Prepaid and other assets	124.0	111.0
Income taxes recoverable	113.5	31.2
Deferred income taxes	10.9	3.8
	3,258.4	3,120.8
Capital assets	544.8	567.1
Goodwill from business combinations	874.5	854.8
Intangible assets	79.0	60.1
Other assets	101.1	83.5
	4,857.8	4,686.3
Liabilities and Shareholders' Equity		
Current liabilities:		
Accounts payable	1,153.3	1,193.6
Accrued liabilities	492.1	487.9
Income taxes payable	119.9	42.7
Deferred income taxes	4.5	1.1
Current portion of long-term debt	0.5	0.6
	1,770.3	1,725.9
Long-term debt	750.9	750.2
Accrued pension and post-employment benefits	76.8	54.9
Deferred income taxes	17.8	47.5
Other long-term liabilities	27.6	13.2
	2,643.4	2,591.7
Shareholders' equity	2,214.4	2,094.6
	4,857.8	4,686.3

CELESTICA INC.
CONSOLIDATED STATEMENTS OF OPERATIONS
(In millions of U.S. dollars, except per share amounts)
Year ended December 31, 2006

	2004	2005	2006
Revenue	8,839.8	8,471.0	8,811.7
Cost of sales	8,431.9	7,989.9	8,359.9
Gross profit	407.9	481.1	451.8
Selling, general & admin expenses	331.6	296.9	285.6
Amortization of intangible assets	34.6	28.4	27.0
Integration costs related to acquisitions	3.1	0.6	0.9
Other charges	603.2	130.9	211.8
Accretion of convertible debt	17.6	7.6	---
Interest on long-term debt	18.7	48.4	67.1
Interest expense (income), net	1.0	(6.2)	(4.5)
Loss before income taxes	(601.9)	(25.5)	(136.1)
Income taxes expense (recovery):			
Current	17.6	36.9	(40.7)
Deferred	234.6	(15.6)	55.2
	252.2	21.3	14.5
Net loss	(854.1)	(46.8)	(150.6)
Basic loss per share	(3.85)	(0.21)	(0.66)
Diluted loss per share	(3.85)	(0.21)	(0.66)
Shares used in computing per share amounts (in millions):			
Basic	222.1	226.2	227.2
Diluted	222.1	226.2	227.2
Net loss in accordance with U.S. GAAP	(867.5)	(42.8)	(149.3)
Basic loss per share	(3.91)	(0.19)	(0.66)
Diluted loss per share,	(3.91)	(0.19)	(0.66)

CELESTICA INC.
CONSOLIDATED STATEMENTS OF CASH FLOWS
(In millions of U.S. dollars)
Year ended December 31, 2006

	2004	2005	2006
Cash provided by (used in):			
Operations:			
Net loss	(854.1)	(46.8)	(150.6)
Items not affecting cash:			
Depreciation and amortization	207.7	152.7	134.2
Deferred income taxes	234.6	(15.6)	55.2
Accretion of convertible debt	17.6	7.6	---
Non-cash charge for option issuances	7.6	9.0	5.1
Restructuring charges	35.3	11.0	47.9
Other charges	482.4	(15.3)	34.6
Gain on settlement of principal component of convertible debt	(32.9)	(13.9)	---
Inventory write-down related to restructuring	61.2	---	---
Other	1.9	14.5	1.9
Changes in non-cash working capital items:			
Accounts receivable	(253.0)	42.0	(24.8)
Inventories	85.6	---	(172.0)
Prepaid and other assets	(12.9)	17.3	2.7
Income taxes recoverable	(50.0)	(24.4)	72.1
Accounts payable and accrued liabilities	(113.8)	51.2	108.0
Income taxes payable	43.6	29.0	(75.1)
Non-cash working capital changes	(300.5)	115.1	(89.1)
Cash provided by (used in) operations	(139.2)	218.3	39.2
Investing:			
Acquisitions, net of cash acquired/indebtedness assumed	(39.6)	(6.5)	(19.1)
Purchase of capital assets	(142.2)	(158.5)	(189.1)
Proceeds, net of cash divested from sale of operations or assets	101.3	50.9	1.0
Other	0.6	2.2	(0.7)
Cash used in investing activities	(79.9)	(111.9)	(207.9)

CELESTICA INC.
CONSOLIDATED STATEMENTS OF CASH FLOWS cont.
(In millions of U.S. dollars)
Year ended December 31, 2006

	2004	2005	2006
Financing:			
Increase in long-term debt 500.0		250.0	---
Long-term debt issue costs . . . .(12.0)		(4.2)	---
Repayment of long-term debt . . . . (41.1)		(3.4)	(0.6)
Deferred financing costs . . . . (4.0)		(1.1)	---
Repurchase of convertible debt . . . .(299.7)		(352.0)	---
Issuance of share capital 14.6		8.0	5.3
Other 1.3		(3.5)	(1.3)
Cash provided by (used in) financing activities 159.1		(106.2)	3.4
Increase (decrease) in cash . . . . (60.0)		0.2	(165.3)
Cash, beginning of year 1,028.8		968.8	969.0
Cash, end of year 968.8		969.0	803.7

Cash is comprised of cash and short-term investments.

Practice Case #3 Answer

Calculations

Accounts Receivable Days

Sales		8,811
1 Day of sales	(8811/365)	24
Accounts receivable ending balance		973
Ending AR balance/1 Day of sales	(973/24)	40
Accounts Receivable Days		**40 days**

Inventory Days

Sales		8,811
1 Day of sales	(8811/365)	24
Inventory ending balance		1,197
Ending inventory balance/1 Day of sales	(1197/24)	50
Inventory Days		**50 days**

Accounts Payable Days

Sales		8,811
1 Day of sales	(8811/365)	24
Accounts payable ending balance		1,193
Ending accounts payable/1 Day of sales	(1193/24)	49
Accounts Payable Days		**49 days**

The cash cycle time is the number days the company takes to recover its cash. For a company that resells inventory, this begins with the day of purchase of the inventory until it is sold (inventory days) and the time it waits for its invoice to be paid (accounts receivable days).

For Celestica, cash cycle time is:

Inventory days	50
Accounts Receivable days	40
Total time cash invested in inventory and accounts receivable	90
LESS	
Accounts Payable days	49
Shortfall	**41 days**

These numbers mean that the company is paying its bills on average in 49 days although it does not recover its cash from operations for 90 days on average, 50 days as inventory and another 40 days to collect the sale.

The notes to the financial statements are too long to include in this book, but can be accessed at www.sedar.com. Notes provide vital clues about the financial condition of the company.

The terms of purchase in the contract electronic industry are on average around 30 days, with close to 60 days being the maximum the company can stretch their suppliers without being cut off. It seems the suppliers are being paid on average shortly before they would have been cut off.

Although cash flow from operations is not positive, it has been improving substantially in the last three years. Restructuring charges often are the result of management's inability to accurately predict the level and type of production necessary to meet future market demand. Typical restructuring charges include write-offs of items that are no longer of value such as obsolete inventory and equipment, redundant staff, and production facilities that are no longer needed, continue to be significant.

The increase in inventory has approximately 7 times the negative effect on cash that the increase in accounts receivable has (172 compared to 25). Although accounts receivable seem under control, the inventory levels do not seem to fit the modest increase in sales. Perhaps the increased inventory is a result of purchase contracts with long-lead times which could not be cancelled. This could be explained by the following: if Celestica ordered custom products from suppliers and could not cancel these orders because the customer cancelled or became insolvent, then the inventory would still arrive. This would help explain the increase in inventory without a corresponding increase in sales and subsequent restructuring charges.

The purchase of capital assets is using up a large amount of cash at a time when sales are not increasing substantially and inventory is up. Perhaps this another instance of commitments made in the past coming home to roost. It may take some time to reverse this trend.

The good news seems to be that the company is not increasing its long-term debt for the first time in 3 years.

Profitability, efficiency, and solvency ratio calculations

Although working through the cash cycle days calculations is enough to give you the answers you need regarding this company, I have included the following profitability, efficiency, and solvency ratio calculations for illustration purposes.

181

Profitability Ratios

Return on sales (Profit Margin) (%)
= Net income after taxes/Net sales X 100
Loss of (150.6)/8811.7 X 100 = - 1.7%
The company was unprofitable in 2006 (as it was in 2005 and 2004).

Return on assets (%)
= Net income after taxes/Total assets X 100
Loss of (150.6)/4686.3 X 100 = - 3.2%
This ratio is negative and reflects the lack of profit from the investment in the company's assets.

Return on Net Worth (return on equity) (%)
= Net income after taxes/ Net worth X 100
Loss of (150.6)/2094.6 X 100 = - 7.2%
This is a negative return on the shareholders' investment and cannot be sustained very long if the company is to survive.

Number of Times Interest is Earned
= Net income before interest and tax/Annual interest expense
(- 150.6 + 67.1 - 4.5 -40.7)/ (67.1 - 4.5) = -2.1 times
This means the losses are 2.1 times the interest the company has to pay.

Gross margin (%)
= Gross profit/Net sales X 100
451.8/8811.7 X 100 = 5.1%
This is very low and leaves very little for expenses and profit.

Solvency ratios

Current ratio
= Total current assets/Total current liabilities
3,120.8/1725.9 = 1.8
This is a healthy ratio. However, a large portion of the current assets is inventory. This might mean that there is obsolescent or slow moving inventory causing a bubble in the inventory number. This is not surprising for a company in the high-tech industry.

Quick ratio
= (Cash + accounts receivable)/Total current liabilities
(803.7 + 973.2)/1725.9 = 1.03
This is ratio should be higher. This confirms that inventory makes up the bulk of the current ratio above.

Total liabilities to net worth (%)
= Total liabilities/Net worth X 100
2591.7/2094.6 X 100 = 123.7%
This ratio is a little too high. The company owes more than what it is worth.

Current liabilities to Net worth (%)
= Total current liabilities/ Net worth X 100
1725.9/2094.6 X 100 = 82.4%
This is much lower than the ratio just above. This indicates that the company is getting long-term financing rather than short-term financing.

Debt to equity
= Notes payable + Current and long-term debt/ Net worth
(0 + 2591.7)/2094.6 = 1.2
This ratio is telling us that debt is slightly higher than equity.
This ratio could be a lending covenant.

Fixed assets to net worth (%)
= Fixed assets/ Net worth X 100
(567.1 + 854.8 + 60.1 + 83.5)/2094.6 X 100 = 74.7%
This means that fixed assets are about 75% of the company's
net worth. The issue here is that Goodwill is by far the largest
part of fixed assets. Goodwill is simply an accounting entry to
reflect how much more the company paid for than the value
of the assets purchased and does not have any tangible worth.
Celestica has made many acquisitions.

Efficiency ratios

Accounts Receivable Turnover
= Net sales/Accounts receivable
8811.7/973.2 = 9 times
This is a healthy turnover of receivables and indicates that
collecting the bills is not a problem.

Days of Sales Outstanding (DSO)
= Accounts receivable/(Sales/365)
973.2/(8811.7/365) = 40.3 days
This is reasonable for this industry.

Inventory Turnover
= Cost of goods sold /Inventory
8359.9/1197.9 = 7
This ratio is a little low. Inventory is turning over more slowly than accounts receivable.

Assets to Net Sales (%)
= Total assets/ Net sales X 100
4686.3/8811.7 X 100 = 53.2%
This ratio means that the company generates about $2 of sales for every dollar invested in its assets, which is low.

Sales to the Net Working Capital
= Net sales/Net working capital
8811.7/(3120.8 -1725.9) = 6.4
This ratio means that the company is producing about $6 of sales for very dollar of working capital, not a surpise given the portion that is inventory.

Accounts Payable to Sales (%)
= Accounts payable/ Net sales X 100
1193.6/8811.7 X 100 = 13.5%
This is a relatively high ratio for the industry and reflects the company's high purchases of inventory.

Conclusion

It seems that management is biting the bullet and is hoping that sales will increase, that they have the right inventory for their future market, will not have any substantial bad debt increases, and will be able to maintain its bank covenants.

In the meantime, investing in Celestica should perhaps be delayed until time proves whether management is correct in its assumptions. Because accounts payable can be stretched at the first sign of a cash shortage, suppliers should consider securing their position before extending or increasing lines of credit.

NOTE: Keep in mind that for these illustration purposes we are working with 2006 financial statements, which do not represent the current financial state of the company.

Practice Case #4 Nortel

21

For this practice case we are using the actual 2006 financial statements of a publicly traded company.

Nortel Networks started out as a telephone manufacturer called Northern Telecom. For much of its history they were considered a blue-chip stock and formed the backbone of many investment funds. However, nothing lasts forever and this company illustrates the importance of never making assumptions based on past reputation.

Because this is a Canadian public company these financial statements are publicly available through **www.sedar.com.** but since they are also have a U.S. presence and are listed on the NASDAQ their financial statements are also available on **www.edgar.com.** There might be some minor differences between these financial statements due to the differences between U.S. and Canadian GAAP, differences that the new International Financial Reporting Standards with soon do away with.

In this particular case, the notes to the financial statements are too large to be included in this book, but they too can be read on-line at www.sedar.com, and at www.edgar.com.

Nortel Networks Inc.
Auditors Report

To the Shareholders and Board of Directors of Nortel Networks Corporation

We have audited the accompanying consolidated balance sheets of Nortel Networks Corporation and subsidiaries ("Nortel") as of December 31, 2006 and 2005 and the related consolidated statements of operations, changes in equity and comprehensive income (loss) and cash flows for each of the three years in the period ended December 31, 2006. These financial statements are the responsibility of Nortel's management. Our responsibility is to express an opinion on these financial statements based on our audits.

We conducted our audits in accordance with Canadian generally accepted auditing standards and the standards of the Public Company Accounting Oversight Board (United States). Those standards require that we plan and perform the audit to obtain reasonable assurance about whether the financial statements are free of material misstatement. An audit includes examining, on a test basis, evidence supporting the amounts and disclosures in the financial statements. An audit also includes assessing the accounting principles used and significant estimates made by management, as well as evaluating the overall financial statement presentation. We believe that our audits provide a reasonable basis for our opinion.

In our opinion, such consolidated financial statements present fairly, in all material respects, the financial position of Nortel as of December 31, 2006 and 2005 and the results of its operations and its cash flows for each of the three years in the period ended December 31, 2006 in conformity with accounting principles generally accepted in the United States of America.

As described in Note 4 to the consolidated financial statements, the accompanying consolidated financial statements of Nortel as of December 31, 2005 and for the years ended December 31, 2005 and 2004 have been restated. We therefore withdraw our previous report dated April 28, 2006 on those financial statements, as originally filed.

We have also audited, in accordance with the standards of the Public Company Accounting Oversight Board (United States), the effectiveness of Nortel's internal control over financial reporting as of December 31, 2006, based on the criteria established in Internal Control -Integrated Framework issued by the Committee of Sponsoring Organizations of the Treadway Commission, and our report dated March 15, 2007 expressed an unqualified opinion on management's assessment of the effectiveness of Nortel's internal control over financial reporting and an adverse opinion on the effectiveness of Nortel's internal control over financial reporting because of a material weakness.

Deloitte & Touche LLP Independent Registered Chartered Accountants

Toronto, Canada
March 15, 2007

NORTEL NETWORKS CORPORATION
Consolidated Statements of Operations
for the year ended December 31, 2006
(Millions of U.S. dollars)

Revenues:	2006	2005	2004
Products	10,158	9,338	8,511
Services	1,260	1,171	967
Total Revenues	11,418	10,509	9,478
Cost of revenues:			
Products	6,267	5,590	5,037
Services	712	641	519
Total cost of revenues	6,979	6,231	5,556
Gross profit	4,439	4,278	3,922
Selling, general & admin. expense	2,503	2,429	2,146
Research and development expense	1,939	1,874	1,975
Amortization of intangibles	26	17	9
In-process research & development exp.	22	---	---
Special charges	105	169	181
(Gain) loss on sale of businesses and assets(a)	(206)	47	(91)
Shareholder litigation settlement exp. (recovery)	(219)	2,474	---
Operating earnings (loss)	269	(2,732)	(298)
Other income - net	212	295	217
Interest expense			
Long-term debt	(272)	(209)	(192)
Other	(68)	(10)	(10)
Earnings (loss) from continuing operations before income taxes, minority interests and equity in net earnings (loss) of associated companies	141	(2,656)	(283)
Income tax benefit (expense)	(60)	81	20
	81	(2,575)	(263)
Minority interests - net of tax	(59)	(39)	(33)
Equity in net earnings (loss) of associated companies - net of tax	(3)	3	---
Net earnings (loss) from continuing operations	19	(2,611)	(296)
Net earnings from discontinued oper.- net of tax	---	1	49
Net earnings (loss) before cum. effect of acctg change	19	(2,610)	(247)
Cum. effect of acctg change - net of tax (note 3)	9	---	---
Net earnings (loss)	28	(2,610)	(247)

NORTEL NETWORKS CORPORATION
Consolidated Statements of Operations (cont.)

	2006	2005	2004
Basic and diluted earnings (loss) per common share			
- from continuing operations	0.06	(6.02)	(0.68)
- from discontinued operations	0.00	0.00	0.11
Basic and diluted earnings (loss) per common share .	0.06	(6.02)	(0.57)

NORTEL NETWORKS CORPORATION
Consolidated Balance Sheets as of December 31, 2006
(Millions of U.S. dollars)

ASSETS	2006	2005
Current assets		
Cash and cash equivalents	3,492	2,951
Restricted cash and cash equivalents	639	77
Accounts receivable - net	2,785	2,826
Inventories - net	1,989	2,080
Deferred income taxes- net	276	377
Other current assets	742	798
Total current assets	9,923	9,109
Investments	204	244
Plant and equipment - net.	1,530	1,560
Goodwill	2,529	2,586
Intangible assets -net.	241	172
Deferred income taxes-net	3,863	3,664
Other assets	689	800
Total assets	18,979	18,135

LIABILITIES AND SHAREHOLDERS' EQUITY

Current liabilities	2006	2005
Trade and other accounts payable	1,125	1,181
Payroll and benefit-related liabilities	640	803
Contractual liabilities	243	348
Restructuring liabilities.	97	99
Other accrued liabilities	4,603	4,232
Long-term debt due within one year	18	1,446
Total current liabilities.	6,726	8,109
Long-term debt	4,446	2,439
Deferred income taxes-net	97	104
Other liabilities	5,810	5,937
Total liabilities	17,079	16,589
Minority interests in subsidiary companies	779	783

NORTEL NETWORKS CORPORATION
Consolidated Balance Sheets as of December 31, 2006 (cont.)
(Millions of U.S. dollars)

	2006	2005
SHAREHOLDERS' EQUITY		
Common shares, without par value		
-Authorized shares: unlimited;		
Issued and outstanding shares:	433,934,747	433,916,293
for 2006 and 2005, respectively 33,938		3,932
Additional paid-in capital 3,378		3,281
Accumulated deficit . . . . (35,574)		(35,602)
Accumulated other comprehensive loss . . . . . . (621)		(848)
Total shareholders' equity 1,121		763
Total liabilities and shareholders' equity 18,979		8,135

NORTEL NETWORKS CORPORATION
Consolidated Statements of Cash Flows
for the year ended December 31, 2006
(Millions of U.S. dollars)

	2006	2005	2004
Cash flows from (used in) operating activities			
Net earnings (loss)	28	(2,610)	(247)
Adjustments to reconcile net earnings (loss) from continuing operations to net cash from (used in) operating activities, net of effects from acquisitions and divestitures of businesses:			
Amortization and depreciation	290	302	341
Non-cash portion of shareholder litigation settlement expense (recovery)	(219)	1,899	---
Non-cash portion of special charges and related asset write downs	3	38	6
Non-cash portion of in-process research and development expense	22	---	---
Equity in net (earnings) loss of associated companies	3	(3)	---
Stock based compensation expense	112	88	77
Deferred income taxes	31	(116)	(47)
Net (earnings) from discontinued operations	---	(1)	(49)
Cumulative effect of accounting change	(9)	---	---
Pension and other accruals	346	299	220
(Gain) loss on sale or write down of investments, businesses and assets	(200)	(20)	(110)
Minority interests	59	39	33
Other - net	220	123	274
Change in operating assets and liabilities	(449)	(217)	(683)
Net cash from (used in) operating activities of continuing operations	237	(179)	(185)

194

Cash flows from (used in) investing activities

Expenditures for plant and equipment . . . .(316)	(258)	(276)
Proceeds on disposals of plant and equipment . 143	10	10
Change in restricted cash and cash equivalents (557)	3	(11)
Acquisitions of investments and businesses - net of cash acquired . . . . . .(146)	(651)	(5)
Proceeds from the sale of investments and businesses 603	470	150
Net cash from (used in) investing activities of continuing operations . . . . (273)	(426)	(132)

Cash flows from (used in) financing activities

Dividends paid by subsidiaries to minority interests (60)	(43)	(33)
Increase in notes payable 105	70	92
Decrease in notes payable . . . . (79)	(83)	(84)
Proceeds from issuance of long-term debt . 3,300	---	---
Repayments of long-term debt . . . . . . (2,725)	---	(107)
Debt issuance cost . . . .(42)	---	---
Increase in capital leases payable 1	---	---
Decrease in capital leases payable . . . .(17)	(10)	(9)
Issuance of common shares 1	6	31
Common share consolidation cost . . . . . . (1)	---	---
Net cash from (used in) financing activities of continuing operations 483	(60)	(110)
Effect of foreign exchange rate changes on cash and cash equivalents 94	(102)	88
Net cash from (used in) continuing operations . 541	(767)	(339)
Net cash from (used in) operating activities of discontinued operations . . . . ---	33	22

Net increase (decrease) in cash and cash equivalents . . . . 541 | (734) | (317)

Cash and cash equivalents

at beginning of year 2,951	3,685	4,002
at end of year. 3,492	2,951	3,685

Practice Case #4 Answer

Calculations

Accounts Receivable Days

Sales		11,418
1 Day of sales:	(11,418/365)	31
Accounts receivable ending balance	2,785	
Ending AR balance/ 1 Day of sales	(2785/31)	89
Accounts Receivable Days		**89 days**

Inventory Days

Sales		11,418
1 Day of sales	(11,418/365)	31
Inventory ending balance		1,989
Ending inventory balance/1 Day of sales	(1989/31)	64
Inventory Days		**64 days**

Accounts Payable Days

Sales		11,418
1 Day of sales:	(11,418/365)	31
Accounts payable ending balance		1,125
Ending accounts payable/1 Day of sales	(1125/31)	36
Accounts Payable Days		**36 days**

The cash cycle time is the number days the company takes to recover its cash. For a company that resells inventory, this begins with the day of purchase of the inventory until it is sold (inventory days) and the time it waits for its invoice to be paid (accounts receivable days).

For Nortel, cash cycle time is:

Inventory days	64
Accounts Receivable Days	89
Total time cash invested in inventory and A/R	153
LESS:	
Accounts Payable days	36
Shortfall	**117 days**

These numbers mean that the company is paying its bills on average in 36 days although it does not recover its cash from operations for 153 days on average, 64 days as inventory and another 89 days to collect the sale.

The notes to the financial statements are too long to include in this book, but can be accessed at www.sedar.com. Notes provide vital clues about the financial condition of the company.

The terms of purchase in the high-tech networking electronic industry are on average around 30 days, with close to 60 days being the maximum the company can stretch their suppliers without being cut off. It seems the suppliers are being paid on average well before they would have been cut off.

For the first time in 3 years, income from operations is positive, although not substantial (28). Shareholder litigation expense is using up valuable cash (219). These actions are a result of shareholders suing the company and its management for delays and other irregularities in financial reporting. Write-downs of business investments, in other words restructuring charges, accounted for a large decrease in cash (200).

In spite of its troubles, Nortel is spending cash. The purchase of capital assets is continuing the 3-year trend of using up a large amount of cash (316) at a time when the company has substantial long-term debt. The change in restricted cash has the largest negative effect on cash (557). This means that Nortel's lenders are insisting that some cash be left on hand to help assure them that payments can and will be made on time and reduce the likelihood of default. Acquisitions cost 146 while investing activities in continuing operations used 273 of cash.

Although net cash has gone up compared to the previous year, the source has been the issuance of long-term debt.

Profitability, efficiency, and solvency ratio calculations

Although working through the cash cycle days calculations is enough to give you the answers you need regarding this company, I have included the following profitability, efficiency, and solvency ratio calculations for illustration purposes.

Profitability Ratios

Return on sales (Profit Margin) (%)
= Net income after taxes/Net sales X 100
28/11,418 X 100 = 0 .2%
The company is generating very little profit.

Return on assets (%)
= Net income after taxes/Total assets X 100
28/18,979 X 100 = 0.1%
There is close to no return on assets.

Return on Net Worth (return on equity) (%)
= Net income after taxes/ Net Worth X 100
28/1121 X 100 = 2.5%

The company is providing only a very small return on net worth. Shareholders would earn more from leaving their money in their bank savings account.

Number of Times Interest is Earned
= Net income before interest and tax/Annual interest expense
(28 + 272+ 68 +60)/(272 + 68) = 428/340 = 1.3

The company earns 1.3 times the amount it pays in interest. This is low.

Gross margin (%)
= Gross profit/Net sales X 100
4439/11,418 X 100 = 38.9%

This means that the company has about $39 from every $100 of sales left over to cover overhead and contribute to profit.

Solvency ratios

Current ratio
= Total current assets/Total current liabilities
9923/6726 = 1.4

This ratio is acceptable but certainly could stand to be higher.

Quick ratio
= (Cash + accounts receivable)/Total current liabilities
(3492 + 639 + 2785)/6726 = 1.0

This is lower than the current ratio and means that they have barely enough working capital to meet their needs.

Total liabilities to net worth (%)
= Total liabilities/Net worth X 100
17,079/1121 X 100 = 1523.6%

This means that liabilities are very high compared to net worth. They are highly leveraged.

Current liabilities to Net worth (%)
= Total current liabilities/ Net worth X 100
6726/1121 X 100 = 600%

This means that current liabilities are 6 times as big as net worth. This is significant because current liabilities have to be paid in the short-term.

Debt to equity
= Notes payable + Current and long-term debt/ Net worth
(0 + 17,079)/1121 = 15.2

This means the company owes 15 times more money than it is worth. It is highly leveraged as evidenced by the interest expense. It is vulnerable to creditors.

Fixed assets to net worth (%)
= Fixed assets/ Net worth X 100
(18,979 - 9923) /1121 X 100 = 807.9%

This means the company's investment in fixed assets is 8 times its net worth, which is very high. They have a lot of overhead.

Efficiency ratios

Accounts Receivable Turnover
= Net sales/Accounts Receivable
11,418/2785 = 4.1

This means that accounts receivable turn over about 4 times a year or about every 90 days. This is slow. It should be 45 to 60 days or less.

Days of Sales Outstanding (DSO)
= Accounts receivable/(Sales/365)
2785/(11,418/365) = 89 days
This ratio is related to accounts receivable ratio and confirms how slow accounts receivable are being collected.

Inventory Turnover
= Cost of goods sold/Inventory
6979/1989 = 3.5 times
This is very low and means the inventory only turns over 3.5 times a year.

Assets to Net Sales (%)
= Total assets/ Net sales X 100
18,979/11,418 X 100 = 166.2%
This is very high and means that the company invests heavily in assets to produce sales.

Sales to the Net Working Capital
= Net sales/Net working capital
11,418/(9923-6726) = 3.6
This means the company is producing $3.6 of sales for every dollar of working capital. The company is not very efficient in its use of working capital.

Accounts Payable to Sales (%)
= Accounts payable/ Net sales X 100
1125/11,418 X 100 = 9.9%
This means the company maintains payables at about 10% of sales. This is acceptable for this industry.

Conclusion

Because Nortel is financing short-term needs with long-term borrowing, it is vulnerable to the demands of its lenders, such as an increase the amount of restricted cash. As long as its lenders continue to let Nortel increase its debt load, the company can try to increase its market share and hope margins and revenues increase while it tries to control its expenses. The speculative investor might gamble on Nortel being able to turn the corner, but the cautious investor will wait for evidence of the turnaround.

NOTE: Keep in mind that for these illustration purposes we are working with 2006 financial statements, which do not represent the current financial state of the company.

On January 14, 2009 Nortel sought bankruptcy protection.

22

Practice Case #5 Wal-Mart

For this practice case we are using the actual financial statements of a publicly traded company.

Wal-Mart Stores Inc. is the undisputed leader in the consumer retail sales industry. Founded by one man, Sam Walton, the company now has the largest number of retail outlets of any company in the world.

You will notice that the company's year end is in January, which is typical of the retail industry. This is the time of year when they have the lowest inventory, the highest cash, and enough time to prepare the financial statements.

Because this is a U.S. public company these financial statements are publicly available through **www.edgar.com.** In this particular case, the notes to the financial statements are too large to be included in this book, but they too can be read on-line at www.edgar.com.

Keep in mind, that for these illustration purposes we are working with 2006 financial statements, which do not represent the current financial state of the company.

Wal-Mart
Auditors Report

The Board of Directors and Shareholders, Wal-Mart Stores, Inc.

We have audited the accompanying consolidated balance sheets of Wal-Mart Stores, Inc. as of January 31, 2007 and 2006, and the related consolidated statements of income, shareholders' equity, and cash flows for each of the three years in the period ended January 31, 2007. These financial statements are the responsibility of the Company's management. Our responsibility is to express an opinion on these financial statements based on our audits.

We conducted our audits in accordance with the standards of the Public Company Accounting Oversight Board (United States). Those standards require that we plan and perform the audit to obtain reasonable assurance about whether the financial statements are free of material misstatement. An audit includes examining, on a test basis, evidence supporting the amounts and disclosures in the financial statements. An audit also includes assessing the accounting principles used and significant estimates made by management, as well as evaluating the overall financial statement presentation. We believe that our audits provide a reasonable basis for our opinion.

In our opinion, the financial statements referred to above present fairly, in all material respects, the consolidated financial position of Wal-Mart Stores, Inc. at January 31, 2007 and 2006, and the consolidated results of its operations and its cash flows for each of the three years in the period ended January 31, 2007, in conformity with U.S. generally accepted accounting principles.

As discussed in Note 13 to the consolidated financial statements, effective January 31, 2007, the Company adopted Statement of Financial Accounting Standards No. 158, Employers' Accounting for Defined Benefit Pension and Other Postretirement Plans.

We also have audited, in accordance with the standards of the Public Company Accounting Oversight Board (United States), the effectiveness of Wal-Mart Stores, Inc.'s internal control over financial reporting as of January 31, 2007, based on criteria established in Internal Control -Integrated Framework issued by the Committee of Sponsoring Organizations of the Treadway Commission and our report dated March 26, 2007 expressed an unqualified opinion thereon.

Rogers, Arkansas
March 26, 2007

Wal-Mart
Consolidated Statements of Income
Fiscal Year Ended January 31 2007

Revenues:	**2007**	**2006**	**2005**
Net sales 344,992		308,945	281,488
Membership and other income 3,658		3,156	2,822
	348,650	312,101	284,310
Costs and expenses:			
Cost of sales 264,152		237,649	216,832
Operating, selling, general and admin. exp. . 64,001		55,739	50,178
Operating income	20,497	18,713	17,300
Interest:			
Debt 1,549		1,171	931
Capital leases .260		249	253
Interest income . . . . (280)		(242)	(204)
Interest, net 1,529		1,178	980
Income from continuing operations before			
income taxes and minority interest 18,968		17,535	16,320
Provision for income taxes:			
Current 6,276		5,932	5,326
Deferred 89		(129)	263
	6,365	5,803	5,589
Income from cont. oper. before minority interest 12,603		11,732	10,731
Minority interest . . . .(425)		(324)	(249)
Income from continuing operations . .12,178		11,408	10,482
Loss from discontinued operations, net of tax . (894)		(177)	(215)
Net income. .11,284		11,231	10,267
Basic net income per common share:			
Basic income per share from cont. operations . 2.92		2.73	2.46
Basic loss per share from discont. operations . .(0.21)		(0.05)	(0.05)
Basic net income per share 2.71		2.68	2.41
Diluted net income per common share:			
Diluted income per share from cont. operations 2.92		2.72	2.46
Diluted loss per share from discont. operations.(0.21)		(0.04)	(0.05)
Diluted net income per share 2.71		2.68	2.41
Weighted-average number of common shares:			
Basic 4,164		4,183	4,259
Diluted 4,168		4,188	4,266
Dividends per common share 0.67		0.60	0.52

Wal-Mart
Consolidated Balance Sheets
January 31, 2007

Assets	2007	2006
Current assets:		
Cash and cash equivalents	7,373	6,193
Receivables	2,840	2,575
Inventories	33,685	31,910
Prepaid expenses and other	2,690	2,468
Current assets of discontinued operations	---	679
Total current assets	46,588	43,825
Property and equipment, at cost:		
Land	18,612	16,174
Buildings and improvements	64,052	55,206
Fixtures and equipment	25,168	22,413
Transportation equipment	1,966	1,744
Property and equipment, at cost	109,798	95,537
Less accumulated depreciation	(24,408)	(20,937)
Property and equipment, net	85,390	74,600
Property under capital lease:		
Property under capital lease	5,392	5,392
Less accumulated amortization	(2,342)	(2,127)
Property under capital lease, net	3,050	3,265
Goodwill	13,759	12,097
Other assets and deferred charges	2,406	2,516
Non-current assets of discontinued operations . . .	---	1,884
Total assets	151,193	138,187

Liabilities and shareholders' equity		
Current liabilities:		
Commercial paper	2,570	3,754
Accounts payable	28,090	25,101
Accrued liabilities	14,675	13,274
Accrued income taxes	706	1,340
Long-term debt due within one year	5,428	4,595
Obligations under capital leases due within one year	285	284
Current liabilities of discontinued operations	---	477
Total current liabilities	51,754	48,825
Long-term debt	27,222	26,429
Long-term obligations under capital leases	3,513	3,667

Wal-Mart
Consolidated Balance Sheets cont.
January 31, 2007

Non-current liabilities of discont. operations . . . . . . ---		129
Deferred income taxes and other 4,971		4,501
Minority interest 2,160		1,465
Commitments and contingencies		
Shareholders' equity:		
Preferred stock ($0.10 par value;		
100 shares authorized, none issued) . . . . ---		---
Common stock ($0.10 par value; 11,000 shares authorized,		
4,131 and 4,165 issued and outstanding at January 31, 2007		
and January 31, 2006, respectively) 413		417
Capital in excess of par value 2,834		2,596
Retained earnings 55,818		49,105
Accumulated other comprehensive income 2,508		1,053
Total shareholders' equity 61,573		53,171
Total liabilities and shareholders' equity 151,193		**138,187**

Wal-Mart
Consolidated Statements of Cash Flows
Fiscal Year Ended January 31 2007

Cash flows from operating activities:	2007	2006	2005
Net income	11,284	11,231	10,267
Loss from discontinued operations, net of tax	894	177	215
Income from continuing operations	12,178	11,408	10,482

Adjustments to reconcile income from continuing operations to net cash provided by operating activities:

	2007	2006	2005
Depreciation and amortization	5,459	4,645	4,185
Deferred income taxes	89	(129)	263
Other operating activities	1,039	613	388

Changes in certain assets and liabilities, net of effects of acquisitions:

	2007	2006	2005
Increase in accounts receivable	(214)	(466)	(302)
Increase in inventories	(1,274)	(1,761)	(2,515)
Increase in accounts payable	2,344	2,425	1,681
Increase in accrued liabilities	588	1,002	997
Net cash provided by operating activities of continuing operations	20,209	17,737	15,179
Net cash used in operating activities of discontinued operations	(45)	(102)	(135)
Net cash provided by operating activities	20,164	17,635	15,044

Cash flows from investing activities:

	2007	2006	2005
Payments for property and equipment	(15,666)	(14,530)	(12,803)
Proceeds from disposal of prop. and equipment	394	1,042	925
Proceeds from disposal of certain international operations, net	610	---	---
Investment in international operations, net of cash acquired	(68)	(601)	(315)
Other investing activities	223	(67)	(99)
Net cash used in investing activities of continuing operations	(14,507)	(14,156)	(12,292)
Net cash provided by (used in) investing activities of discontinued operations	44	(30)	(59)
Net cash used in investing activities	(14,463)	(14,186)	(12,351)

Wal-Mart
Consolidated Statements of Cash Flows cont.
Fiscal Year Ended January 31 2007

Cash flows from financing activities:	2007	2006	2005
(Decrease) increase in commercial paper	(1,193)	(704)	544
Proceeds from issuance of long-term debt	7,199	7,691	5,832
Dividends paid	(2,802)	(2,511)	(2,214)
Payment of long-term debt	(5,758)	(2,724)	(2,131)
Purchase of Company stock	(1,718)	(3,580)	(4,549)
Payment of capital lease obligations	(340)	(245)	(204)
Other financing activities	(227)	(349)	113
Net cash used in financing activities	(4,839)	(2,422)	(2,609)
Effect of exchange rate changes on cash	97	(101)	205
Net increase in cash and cash equivalents	959	926	289
Cash and cash equivalents at beginning of year 1	6,414	5,488	5,199
Cash and cash equivalents at end of year 2	7,373	6,414	5,488

Supplemental disclosure of cash flow information:

Income tax paid	6,665	5,962	5,593
Interest paid	1,553	1,390	1,163
Capital lease obligations incurred	159	286	377

Practice Case #5 Answer

Calculations

Accounts Receivable Days

Sales		348,650
1 Day of sales	(348,650/365)	955
A/Receivable ending balance:		2840
Ending AR balance/1 Day of sales	(2840/955)	3
Accounts Receivable Days		**3 days**

Inventory Days

Sales		348,650
1 Day of sales	(348,650/365)	955
Inventory ending balance		33,685
Ending inventory balance/1 Day of sales	(33,685/955)	35
Inventory Days		**35 days**

Accounts Payable Days

Sales		348,650
1 Day of sales	(348,650/365)	955
Accounts payable ending balance		28,090
Ending accounts payable/1 Day of sales	(28,090/955)	29
Accounts Payable Days		**29 days**

The cash cycle time is the number days the company takes to recover its cash. For a company that resells inventory, this begins with the day of purchase of the inventory until it is sold (inventory days) and the time it waits for its invoice to be paid (accounts receivable days).

For Wal-Mart, Cash cycle time is:

Inventory days	35
Accounts Receivable Days	3
Total time cash invested in inventory and A/R:	38
LESS:	
Accounts Payable days	29
Shortfall	**9 days**

These numbers mean that the company is paying its bills on average in 29 days although it recovers its cash from operations in 38 days on average, 35 days as inventory and another 3 days to collect the sale.

The notes to the financial statements are too long to include in this book, but because this is U.S. publicly traded company they can be accessed at www.edgar.com. Notes provide vital clues about the financial condition of the company.

The terms of purchase in the "Big Box" retail industry are on average between 30 days and 60 days, with some seasonal purchases with extended terms, such as summer season items, and winter clothing. Because of its size, and its ability to pay and good payment record, Wal-Mart is able to negotiate not only favorable terms, but also very competitive prices, especially from foreign manufacturers and suppliers.

Its continuing expansion (now over 2200 stores, making it the largest retailer in the world) explains Wal-Mart's large investment in Property and Equipment as evidenced by the large amount in the "Investing Activities" section of the statement of changes in financial position. Almost 80% of the expansion is provided by the excellent cash flow from operations.

Profitability, efficiency, and solvency ratio calculations

Although working through the cash cycle days calculations is enough to give you the answers you need regarding this company, I have included the following profitability, efficiency, and solvency ratio calculations for illustration purposes.

Profitability Ratios

Return on sales (Profit Margin) (%)
= Net income after taxes/Net sales X 100
11,284/344,992 X 100 = 3.3%
This is a good margin for the retail industry. Because sales volume is large, the dollar value of their profit margin is very significant.

Return on assets (%)
= Net income after taxes/Total assets X 100
11,284/151,193 X 100 = 7.5%
This is a very good return for the industry and applies to a large dollar amount of assets.

Return on Net Worth (return on equity) (%)
= Net income after taxes/ Net worth X 100
11,284/61,573 X 100 = 18.3%
The company produces a very good return given the amount of shareholder investment.

Number of Times Interest is Earned
= Net income before interest and tax/Annual interest expense
(11,284 +1529 + 6365)/1529 = 12.5
This means that it only takes about a month's sales to pay for interest and taxes. This is very good.

Gross margin (%)
= Gross profit/Net sales X 100
(348,650 - 264,152)/344,992 X 100 = 24.5 %
This is very high for the retail industry. The company has about 75% of every sale left over from sales to pay for expenses and provide a profit. This reflects the company's ability to buy inventory at advantageous prices.

Solvency ratios

Current ratio
= Total current assets/Total current liabilities
46,588/51,754 = 0.9
Current assets are lower than current liabilities. This usually would be a problem, but this company's size means that this ratio is adequate. Their payables to suppliers can probably be stretched out when necessary without impeding their ability to get inventory, and inventory that is not selling will be returned for a full credit.

Quick ratio
= (Cash + accounts receivable)/Total current liabilities
(7373 + 2840)/ 51,754 = 0.20
This is low, but sustainable for a company of this size. The majority of its current assets are inventory and, because its sells to the public at retail, its accounts receivable are low.

Total liabilities to net worth (%)
= Total liabilities/Net worth X 100
(151,193 - 61,573)/61,573 X 100 = 145.6%
Liabilities are high but not unusual for a retail giant. The size of shareholder investment and high retained earnings makes this position acceptable.

Current liabilities to Net worth (%)
= Total current liabilities/ Net worth X 100
51,754//61,573 X 100 = 84.1%
This means that current liabilities are covered easily by net worth and that the company is not relying on debt financing to pay its bills.

Debt to equity
= Notes payable + Current and long-term debt/ Net worth
(0 + (151,193 - 61,573)/ 61,573 = 1.5
This is the same as total liabilities to net worth because there are no notes payable. Although "commercial paper" is listed, there is no confirmation that this item represents notes payable. Even if it is, the amount of 2570 would not have a significant impact.

Fixed assets to net worth (%)
= Fixed assets/ Net worth X 100
(151,193 - 46,588)/ 61,573 X 100 = 169.9%
The company has a high amount of fixed assets which is not surprising given the size and number of its stores, warehouses, trucks and other equipment.

Efficiency ratios

Accounts Receivable Turnover
= Net sales/Accounts receivable
344,992/2840 = 121.5
This is excellent and not a surprise as they sell for cash or by credit card which settles in about 2 to 3 days.

Days of Sales Outstanding (DSO)
= Accounts receivable/(Sales/365)
2840/(348,650/365) = 3.0 days
This confirms the accounts receivable turnover. The company gets its cash almost immediately.

Inventory Turnover
= Cost of goods sold/Inventory
264,152/33,685 = 7.8
This means inventory turns over about 8 times a year or about every 45 days.

Assets to Net Sales (%)
= Total assets/ Net sales X 100
151,193/344,992 X 100 = 43.8%
This is very good and means that there is about $2 of sales for every dollar invested in assets.

Sales to the Net Working Capital
= Net sales/Net working capital
344,992/(46,588 -51,754) = -66.7
This means that the company is producing a large volume of sales in spite of slightly negative working capital. This is acceptable because of the company's size and its ability to return goods that are not selling to suppliers.

Accounts Payable to Sales (%)
= Accounts payable/ Net sales X 100
28,090/344,992 X 100 = 8.1%
This means that accounts payable are low in comparison to sales. This indicates the company manages its payables and inventory well.

Conclusion

Strong sales, excellent inventory management, and almost no receivables to collect, have provided Wal-Mart the cash to expand and become the undisputed leader in the consumer retail sales industry. The only limit is Wal-Mart's ability to successfully manage its cash flow as it grows even larger.

NOTE: Keep in mind that for these illustration purposes we are working with 2006 financial statements, which do not represent the current financial state of the company.

Index

A

B

C

219

About the Author

Mike Morley is a Certified Public Accountant (Illinois) who holds the top credit designations in the United States (CCE), Canada (CCP), and the U.K. (MICM). He is an internationally recognized authority in the field of finance with more than 25 years experience in credit, and collections.

A consultant, speaker, and author, his books and articles on business and finance have been published in the USA, Canada, the UK, and Australia.

Mike helps companies with cash flow problems get back on track. He also helps companies through the Sarbanes-Oxley implementation process by designing and testing internal controls in particular those related to credit and accounts receivable.

Mike can be reached by phone at **416-275-1278**, or by email at **mike@mikemorley.com**.

www.mikemorley.com

Other books by Mike Morley

"Sarbanes-Oxley Simplified" revised 2nd edition

ISBN 978-0-9783939-5-3 This book describes, in plain language, what the U.S. Sarbanes-Oxley Act says, it explains why the Act came into effect, and shows what companies need to do to ensure that they are in compliance with the Act.

Revised 2nd Edition!

Sarbanes-Oxley Simplified

1) Is it accurate?

2) Are you sure?

3) Can you prove it?

Mike Morley C.P.A.

IFRS Simplified

A fast and easy to understand overview of the new

International Financial Reporting Standards

Mike Morley C.P.A.

"IFRS Simplified"

ISBN 978-0-9783939-1-5 Like it or not, International Financial Reporting Standards (IFRS) are coming and they will completely change how companies report their financial statements ... Are you ready? If you need to get up to speed fast regarding IFRS then this is the book for you!

LaVergne, TN USA
16 December 2009
167171LV00004B/40/P